Beale Poste

# A Vindication of the Celtic Inscriptions on Gaulish and British Coins

Beale Poste

**A Vindication of the Celtic Inscriptions on Gaulish and British Coins**

ISBN/EAN: 9783337295196

Printed in Europe, USA, Canada, Australia, Japan

Cover: Foto ©ninafisch / pixelio.de

More available books at **www.hansebooks.com**

A

# VINDICATION

OF THE

# CELTIC * INSCRIPTIONS

On Gaulish and British Coins;

WITH

VIGNETTES, AND A PLATE OF FAC-SIMILES OF CHARACTERS USED IN ROMAN

WRITING IN THE FIRST CENTURY, FROM POMPEII.

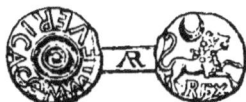

By  BEALE  POSTE.

LONDON:
PRINTED  BY  T.  RICHARDS.
M.DCCC.LXII.

# PREFACE.

SEVERAL literary enigmas of great moment have been solved within the last century. The key to the Egyptian hieroglyphics has been obtained. The arrow-headed writing of the east has been read; and the inscriptions of Persepolis and the Assyrian marbles have been decyphered: and the Phœnician speeches inserted in the play called the *Pœnulus*, that is, the "Carthaginian" of the old Roman comedian Plautus, have been shown to be in close affinity with the Gaelic, or modern Irish language.

Celtic inscriptions on ancient moneys, only seem to remain, as supplying much chance of further literary development, which, as far as they can be decyphered, have the appearance of being of high ethnological interest, in illustrating the habits and customs and the political ideas and biasses of the ancient Celts, both in this country and on the continent.

The Welsh, Irish, and Bretons represent the Celts at the present day; but this same Celtic race once held possession of the whole of Great Britain and Ireland in the time of Julius Cæsar, and the inscriptions of numerous specimens of their coins when correctly read, are found to apply to various chiefs and kings reigning in this our native land, mentioned by the old Roman historians, Dion Cassius, Tacitus, and Suetonius, and in one instance, as is supposed by Cæsar himself.

The Celts used Roman characters in their coinage, as it should be noted; rarely Greek.

The political style and tone of the ancient Gaulish and British chiefs are given out plainly enough by our Celtic coin inscriptions. While Villemarqué's *Gododin*, and the other Celtic poems in his

*Bardes Bretons du Sixième Siècle,* may be referred to, to show
their usual bearing and demeanour among their adherents and com-
rades, in their every day's intercourse among themselves; though
indeed more particularly in war; for, unfortunately, from the un-
quietness of the early part of the middle ages, war became their
principal occupation; and very especially so in this island.

There thus seems no apology required for attending to this
branch of literature—the Celtic inscriptions on ancient Gaulish and
British coins, which even now, though somewhat late in the nine-
teenth century, may be considered to open an almost new field of
inquiry.

A great object being to secure inquirers on these topics from errors,
the caution given in the *Celtic Inscriptions,* on the head of forgery,
may, with advantage, be referred to here. It has been known of
late years, that surmises on the new reading of a type, though only,
perhaps, ventilated in some journal or periodical, have taken shortly
afterwards a more solid form, and that coins conformably inscribed,
have been on sale a few months afterwards. Also, I have known a
coin to appear, the legend of which bore evidence of being mainly
formed from a fac-simile which I myself had published.

I have fully made up my mind to one thing, that though there
may have been controversies going on upon various points connected
with ancient Britain, and in several of which, I have been neces-
sitated in various researches to take a part; yet I will continue the
custom I have always adopted, to disclaim all controversial bias.
My object is solely truth; and I am equally as willing to do
justice to those who have been my opponents, as to those who may
have coincided with me. I accordingly will know no partiali-
ties or repugnancies : and if anyone be conscious that he has, at
any time, made me the object of attack, he will find no difference
made on that account, either in my referring to his numismatic pro-
ductions, whatever they may have been, as points in question may
require, or in giving the meed of approbation, if it be properly due.

# CONTENTS.

# WOODCUTS, Etc.

## PLATE FROM POMPEIAN INSCRIPTIONS.
### *To face the Title.*

# A VINDICATION

OF THE

# CELTIC INSCRIPTIONS.

Fair criticism is a boon to the public, and should be acquiesced in by those who are the objects of it, from the benefits it confers on the community: but if criticism puts on a calumnious garb, or is used as a vehicle of detraction from any sinister motive, unfair criticism of this class should be met with a deserved refutation.

It is on this principle that I now reply to various disparagements of the Celtic Inscriptions which have appeared in the *Literary Gazette* of the 5th October, 1861, and a great portion of them almost in the same words in the *Athenæum* published on the same day: both having been apparently inserted, not by the love of truth, but by the malevolence of one and the same person, or otherwise, as I may presume, under the same combination and direction; so that, considering the two attacks of the same concoction, I reply accordingly. The same sentiments, indeed, are fully participated in, and adopted in both articles.

Were the critic who has the bad taste to assume a very overbearing and pretentious tone in both journals really acquainted with the subject of Gaulish and British coins, I do believe that he would have hailed the appearance of the work of the Celtic Inscriptions with favour and approbation, and held out the right hand of brotherhood; or at any rate on my part there would have been more satisfaction in tolerating his dogmatizing decisions, and more resignation under his magisterial censures: but the ignorance of this critic is truly deplorable; and the wonder is that he should venture to take up the pen on a subject he

B

so little understands—on which, indeed, he has nothing to say except the most trivial common-places ; also that he should cite so familiarly authors whom it is evident he is so little acquainted with ; for instance, Duchalais and Lelewel. He seems to suppose that the former wrote on a subject pretty much the same as my own, that is, Celtic Inscriptions (*Literary Gazette*, p. 319, col. 2) ; while as to the latter, he is entirely ignorant that the adjective form of the titular names of the Gaulish chiefs is almost the leading topic of his learned work,—as seems, indeed, admitted by every other English and French numismatic writer. Notwithstanding which, our critic throws it in my teeth, that the same is "one of my inventions;" and pronounces the idea absurd (*Literary Gazette*, p. 320, col. 1, and *Athenæum*, p. 440, col. 3). I will accordingly commence with this topic, and a little reference to Lelewel will show the state of the case.

The critic cannot more effectually injure his own cause, and refute himself, than by this his erroneous assertion with respect to the style assumed by the chiefs and potentates of ancient Gaul in their inscriptions on their moneys. We have two passages to examine in Lelewel to clear up the point, *i. e.* those at pp. 236 and 316 of his *Type Gaulois*, and he is decisive authority in this matter.

Lelewel, in the first passage referred to, speaking of the adjuncts Remos, Santonos, Turonos, Sotiota, &c., to names, as in Atisios Remos, Arivos Santonos, Cantorix Turonos, Adietuanus Sotiota, &c., says that they, that is, the said adjuncts, are not so much the names of places as the epithets of the chiefs—in fact the chiefs themselves. His words are: "Ce n'est pas le nom de lieu, mais c'est l'épithète du chef, c'est le chef lui-même. Atisius Remus, Arivus Santonus, Cantorix Turonus, Donnus Durnacus, Adietuanus Sotiota, Indutilil Germanus, denotent: gouverneur Remois d'origine, Sotiate, Germain d'origine, de naissance. Par consequent la monnaie inscrite simplement Santonus, Remus, fait sous entendre, chef non nommé, frappant la monnaie." In the second passage, that at p. 316, he says, as I may here give in a translated form: "Certain of the magistrates (des magistrats) inscribed the names of various localities; they inscribed their own proper names, but changing the name of the people for their own patronymics. (Ils inscrivaient leur propres noms changeant le nom du peuple en leur patronimique.") " Thus," he continues, " monetary inscriptions began to show the individualities of the chiefs as possessing sovereign powers. For example, it is Adietuanus Sotiota, that is, the Sotian (Sotianus) who strikes the money, and not the Sotiates, or the population of the tribe so called who do so. At another time it is an anonymous person, a Mantubinus, a Kaletedus who coins it, to whom the money is thus ascribed, and not to the tribes themselves." So far Lelewel acquaints us on this subject; and he adds, that it was only some few, or in other words the states of ancient Gaul of the greater magnitude that did not adopt this rule (*ibid.*)

I have dilated a little on the above topic, as, this objection of our critic being answered, his principal attack falls at once to the ground ; while, on the other hand, had he made this point good, and shown that the names of the Gaulish chiefs are not titular, I should have indeed been guilty of mere invention, and unworthy of the confidence of the public.

The eyes of our critic may now perhaps become a little opened, and he may begin to see that if the names of the Gaulish chiefs are titular, it is probable that those of Britain may be so likewise, as they were both Celtic nations. He certainly should have ascertained this point first, before commencing his attack. However, now to proceed to another matter.

The critic objects to my views with regard to the word TASCIOVANTIS; in answer to which I have to observe, that I have explained it on the basis that the Celts of the coining age, both in Gaul and Britain, evidently out of subserviency to the Romans, subjoined Latin inflexions and terminations to Celtic words. Thus we have VERCO-BRETO and COSII on the Continent, and CVNOBELINI, CAMVLODVNO, and TASCIOVANI in Britain, and other instances. Following out this analogy, the word *Tasciovantis* would appear to correspond with the Roman word *imperantis*, a participle of the present tense ; and such I judge it to have been, as we have no reason to suppose that the use of Latin inflexions and terminations adopted by the Celts was confined to nouns and adjectives only, but that it extended to verbs also.

Latin inflexions are still in use in the German language
in various words adopted from the Latin, as any one may
easily ascertain. I remember that when abroad formerly,
I used to see with much surprise the words "das publi-
cum, dem publico," &c. &c., on the German playbills of
theatrical performances.

Cunobeline, then, borrowed inflexions from the Latin,
and, as appears from his coins, rather copiously so; but
we know not what he borrowed in words, for the term
REX, which occurs on his moneys, and which might easily
be mistaken for pure Latin, is Celtic also, and occurs in
numerous dialects of that language, ancient and modern,
in the forms REX, RIXS, RIX, REIX, REICHS, VRAGH, RIG,
RIGH, and RI, as appears from *Lelewel* and other authorities.
See also Villemarqué's Dissertation *Sur l'Inscription de
Lomarec*, 4to, 1858, p. 16. Indeed it is most probable,
that the Romans borrowed the word from the ancient
Celts.

There is not any language on authentic British coins
to my knowledge, always excepting inflexions, but the
Celtic. There is not one word upon them which is exclusively Latin. There is not even the Latin " et " for " and."
For when this conjunction would appear to be used, it
seems it is the Celtic " a " which is brought forward, as
in the inscription on one of the coins of the Southern
Belgæ, or Firbolgi; which is considered to read, VERIC A
COMMI(OS) F(IRBOLG); that is, " Vericus and the Community of the Firbolgi." (See *Celt. Insc.* pp. 43, 44.)

Cunobeline's use of Latin, whether it extended further
than inflexions or no, should least of all surprise an
Englishman, seeing we borrow so much in words from the
same language, though not indeed of inflexions of nouns
and adjectives, which, according to the genius of our language, are best supplied by prepositions; nor do we either
take inflexions of participles from them. We also borrow
much from the Greek and French. But not to go into extraneous matters further than required. Let the critic,
then, not despise Cunobeline and his British population
that they began transplanting Latin inflexions into their
own tongue, and thus put themselves in the road of progress to a higher level of civilization: particularly as it is
to be recollected that they had before no inflexions in

their Celtic speech of that day, as I have shown in two or three passages of the " Celtic Inscriptions," and more at length in the *Britannia Antiqua*, pp. 196-7, but spoke a language solely composed of idioms.

To revert to other topics in continuing my answer to the remarks in the two journals. The etymologies of the words ATEVLA and BELATVCADER, the first of which occurs on a coin, the second on lapidary inscriptions, were not given to supply new readings of those words, as is asserted by our critic (see *Lit. Gaz.*, p. 320, cols. 1, 2, and *Athenæum*, p. 440, col. 3, for the first of the above words), but are brought forward as explanations only, of those terms as we have them from the eminent French numismatist, M. De Saulcy.

It will make the objections of our pseudo-critic more intelligible, as also it will do his frequent mistakes, if it be first stated that he wishes the ancient British coinage to be viewed as no more than a degenerate offset and prolongation of the Roman imperial coinage. This is his idea, notwithstanding that Strabo shows us in his *Geography*, book iv, that the islanders entered into treaties with Augustus, and that Tacitus acquaints us in his *Life of Agricola*, c. xiii, that the above-named emperor considered it a *consilium*, that is, "a judicious act," to make no conquests in Britain, and that his successor Tiberius viewed it to be a *præceptum*, or "sacred precept," not to do so. In fact there was not, from the time of Cæsar's second expedition down to the time of Aulus Plautius's invasion, a single Roman soldier hostilely in Britain for nearly a hundred years. Now that the critic's views in these matters are plainly shown to be erroneous, and that it is come to the point that the ancient British coinage as being struck by a Celtic nation then independent is evidently something much more characteristic of those who issued it than he had before in anywise supposed, he seems quite suddenly to have taken the alarm, and almost to make the menace of relinquishing all attention to it. He now says: "If this be a true description," namely, that the legends of Cunobeline's coinage are in the Celtic language, "the sooner (these) numismatic studies are given up the better." (*Athenæum*, p. 440, col. 3, at the end.)

After this it may not be surprising to say that he shows

himself entirely ignorant of the Greek language in his remarks on the word "laos" (*Literary Gazette*, p. 320, col. 2),
a word of occurrence as joined to proper names in the
coins of the Celtico-Greek population near Marseilles, im-
plying "people," that is, "race," in the same sense as
various ancient clans, as the Heraclidæ, and Peleidæ, and
others were designated in ancient times. This word, indeed, is extremely suitable to be used familiarly, as it appears to have been for the purpose.

The critic appears to object to the idea of Greek letters
and a Greek word being introduced in the said legend, in
which the word "laos" forms part of a titular name (*Lit.
Gaz. loco citato*); in answer to which I will just ask the plain
question, As Greek actually is introduced on the Gaulish coins of Gallia Narbonensis, as is universally allowed,
and mixed with the Celtic in their inscriptions, would the
critic himself really wish them explained on any other
principle? Would he explain them on the principle that
the Sclavonian was mixed with their legends, or the Hin-
dostanee? I mention this to show that we must explain
the inscriptions on our Celtic coins as we find them, and
not from preconceived ideas in our own minds. The fact
is, that Greek colonies settled in that part of Gaul as
early as 600 years before the Christian era, and that the
Greek language never thoroughly wore out there during
the coining period. It has since glided into the Provençal,
and now into the modern French.

But to recur to the topic of the transfer of inflexions of
words from one language to another in those days. It
may be required to mention that both Latin and Greek
inflexions were introduced into the Gaulish coinage, as in
the words Lexovio, Cosii, Durnacos Durnocou, and doubt-
less some others, as is admitted by Lelewel in his *Type
Gaulois*, p. 237, and not denied by any one.

He objects, he says (*Athenæum*, p. 440, col. 3), to the
idea of the names of the chiefs in the Gaulish coinage
being believed to be conveyed, in some cases, in one single
word of titular import, as CINGETORIX, king, and VERCIN-
GETORIX, high king; but such, Lelewel expressly tells us,
in his page 316, was the custom in some of the larger
states of Gaul.

Regarding discussions and explanations on the rather

extensive subjects of the legends COMMIUS, TASCIOVANUS,
and FIRBOLG, the space I assign myself will not allow me
to enter upon these topics in these pages ; and it seems
the less required, as the remarks of the critic in both
journals appear to be rather vague and indefinite. I therefore refer on these heads to the "Celtic Inscriptions"
themselves, where I trust the reader will find the matters
in question treated of with all due candour, and a proper
amount of research. I will just say that as far as the
legend TASC· FIR· is concerned, I have found it very plainly
inscribed, with the last word having the orthography of
FIR on Mr. Wigan's coin and on Lord Braybrooke's first
coin, as verified by a good plaster cast. Our critic, however, asserts that all other numismatists besides myself
read FIL, and not FIR (*Literary Gazette*, p. 320, col. 3);
but, contrary to this, I have shown in the *Atlas*, p. 6 of
the Remarks, that many of the most celebrated numismatists in the kingdom do not do so. Another thing I
will also just remark, *en passant*, in answer to a cavil inserted in the *Literary Gazette*, p. 320, col. 3, and in the
*Athenæum*, p. 441, col. 1. It is as to whether Cunobeline
did or did not reign over the people called Belgæ or Firbolgi in this country. In the first passage it is said that
" Cunobeline never reigned over any population who could
reasonably be called the Belgæ ;" in the second, "Cunobeline had nothing to do with the Belgæ, and never could
have ruled over any of their tribes."

In considering this question, it must be remembered
that there were three nations having that denomination
in ancient Britain, as is ascertained by a comparison of
the Welsh *Historical Triads* with the *Commentaries* of
Julius Cæsar, and is not denied by Thierry, and other
writers of eminence. The first, beginning from the South,
were the Belgæ Proper, inhabiting Hampshire, Wiltshire,
Berkshire, Surrey, Sussex, Kent, Dorsetshire, &c. But
these may be considered as out of the question, as they
were more or less independent in those days, and indeed
are believed to have formed a confederation of states, or a
species of Helvetic league or republic among themselves.
(See *Celtic Inscriptions*, chap. vii.) Next to these were
the Midland Belgæ, occupying from the Thames northward to the Stour ; a river forming the northern boundary

of Essex; and north of them the Iceni in their various states, occupying from the said Stour to the Humber. However, these last again, as under another sovereign, were independent, and out of the present question also. So that only the Midland Belgæ remain. Here we come to the point; and that Cunobeline did reign over the Midland Belgæ I think is pretty clear from Cæsar's *Commentaries, Gaulish Wars*, v. 10. He says in that passage, " Maritima pars ab iis incolitur qui prædæ et belli inferendi causâ ex Belgis transierant." In English,—"The maritime part of Britain is inhabited by those who came over from Belgium for the sake of plunder and invasion." The Trinobantes, or inhabitants of Essex, must have been, therefore, a maritime state, and the Iceni north of them the same; as much so as the Cantii south of both.

In regard to certain modern writers, as the two O'Connors, namely, Dr. Charles O'Conor, the translator and editor of the *Rerum Hibernicarum Scriptores*, and O'Connor whose name is connected with the *Chronicles of Eri*, O'Flaherty the Irish historian, Sir William Betham, and Dr. Thackeray, views are ascribed to me for which there is not the slightest foundation. For instead of being the bigoted admirer of these writers, or any of them, as our critic represents, or forming the framework of my system from such sources, I have merely spoken of these persons critically, or quoted some of them casually as writers connected with some portion or other of my work. So much for this one specimen of misrepresentation of our critic; but his other misrepresentations, I am sorry to say, either from his carelessness, or want of experience as a writer, or from some other cause not known to me, are very numerous.

Our critic, among the variety of his objections, does not appear quite to have reconciled himself to the use of the word "community"; in Greek, κοινος, as applied to provinces in the ancient times of the Roman empire (*Athenæum*, p. 441, col. 1). We have, however, Eckhel's opinion on this head, that it was so, in his *Doctrina Nummorum*, vol. vi, p. 245, as also that of Lelewel in his *Type Gaulois*, p. 368, and numerous examples in the Roman-Oriental imperial coinage, as the coin inscribed TO ΚΟΙΝΟΝ ΚΥΠΡΟΥ, and that bearing the legend TO ΚΟΙΝΟΝ ΙΣΙΟΥΝΙΑΣ.

Indeed, as provinces governed by native rulers had, to a certain degree, their own laws, customs, magistracy, and other combinations of their own, it follows that they must have had some familiar term by which they designated themselves in their political position and institutions, in contradistinction to the other phase of their circumstances of being Roman imperial provinces, whether proconsular or senatorial. That term appears to have been in Greek κοινος, and in Celtic commios, and in Latin commvnitas.

The important coin of Augustus, *Vaillant*, vol. ii, p. 35, recording the dedication of a temple to that emperor, and inscribed com(mvnitates) asiæ romæ et avgvsto, shows that Eckhel is right.

It may appear, to some persons, a ready means of over-throwing an opponent, to misrepresent what he says. It is true it does not usually so well answer in the end, and the doing so is the sure sign of a losing game. As to how it affects in the present case, beyond the instance above mentioned, I find that, of about sixty or seventy references and quotations, in both journals, a great proportion of them are incorrect, either in suppressing some explanation or leaving out essential words, so as to make the passages referred to to express mere blunders, or to be without any due application, force, or cogency. For instance (see the *Literary Gazette*, p. 320, col. 2), in the word αстιкo(s), on a coin connected with the neighbourhood of Marseilles, where the Greek language was much in use, it is not mentioned that the c in the legend, though stated just before in the work itself, is one of the *Greek forms* of the letter s, consequently, that the inscription on the coin is actually αстιкos, "native"; that is, according to the rules of the Gaulish coinage, laid down by Lelewel and others, which are fully correct, and which it is in vain for our critic to oppose, it is tantamount to "Native Magistrate," *i. e.* the person who inscribed his titular appellation on the coin. I may here, by the way, observe in illustration of this great use of Greek in the province of Gallia Narbonensis, that the legend ι ϝ ι τ λ s, on the coins of that region and district (see Lelewel's *Type Gaulois*, p. 274, and plate ix, figs. 1, 2, 3), is evidently to be interpreted in the sense of "dependent prince" or

" ruler," its etymology being deducible from the Greek word ὑφίημι, to be " subject to."

I must here, likewise, express an opinion that the c in the inscription on a coin of the EDVI, so learnedly explained by Lelewel and Duchalais as meaning " subordinate" or "native magistrate," should preferably be read as having the power of an s, and that the word is properly AMBASTVS and not AMBACTVS, as being derived from "astikos " in the Greek.

Again, in regard to M. de la Saussaye's important explanation of the word *Belatucader* (*Literary Gazette*, p. 320, col. 2), *i. e.* Mars, whose name I find I have, by inadvertence, omitted to connect with it ; he does not express my meaning, that the word Baal or Bel signifies, in a general sense, " lord," *i. e.* divinity, and only occasionally a specific " divinity," as Apollo in the west, and Jupiter in east, or any other divinity elsewhere. This, however, is necessary to be stated, in order to understand the explanation ; but is omitted to be so.

With regard to the coins of Dubnovellaunos, identified by Mr. Birch, being, in fact, no other than those of Togodubnus, son of Cunobeline (*Literary Gazette*, p. 320, col. 3, and *Athenæum*, p. 441, col. 2), as stated by me (*Celtic Inscriptions, passim*), the critic should have given my reasons, which are the *entire* similarity of style with those attributable to Adminius, and the emblems, &c., being nearly the same ; this may perhaps be a sufficient indication (see *Remarks*, in the *Atlas of Coins*, p. 8).

Added to this, I find reason to complain, on the part of the critic, of an absolute want of attention to matters of fact. I am accused of giving the important inscription of VREIS BOD TASCIA, as VRE-RCI (*Athenæum*, p. 441, col. 1), in reference to which, I must be allowed to say, that such an assertion is not true ; the said words not being of occurrence in the whole volume, and I having referred to it four or five time in it, and always in the correct form. In the like manner, it is not true that I apply the title *fircobretus* to Cunobeline, as said *(Athenæum*, p. 441, col. 1), and that word also does not occur in the volume any more than the two words in the former case. It is likewise, not true that I mistake a horse's legs for letters, in the coin reading QVANGETH, as the critic asserts *(Literary Gazette*, p. 320, col. 3, and *Athenæum*, p. 441, col. 2), as the letters are remarkably clear and distinct; but this coin I will refer to again.

Take another instance of misrepresentation : in translating the Celtic word *tasciovanus*, by the nearest corresponding latin word "imperator," I expressly qualified my doing so, by saying that I meant " imperator " in its original and restricted sense only, as " commander," and not in its subsequently enlarged sense, as adopted by the rulers of Rome, as Emperor, and, as now, connected with imperial sway. I repeated this distinction and qualification several times in the *Celtic Inscriptions ;* yet, notwithstanding, our critic says, in the *Literary Gazette*, p. 320, col. 3, and twice in p. 441, col. 1, of the *Athenæum*, that I pronounce Cunobeline to have had the title of " Emperor of the Belgæ," that is, of the Belgæ of Britain ; the opportunity, I suppose, being too good to be lost, of an attempt at the burlesque.

Our pseudo-critic labours most assiduously to lower the authority of the *Celtic Inscriptions*, as a work of reference (see *Literary Gazette*, p. 319, col. 3). However, the pains taken to collect the most accurate facts relating to the ancient British coinage, and to the kings, states, and chiefs whose names are displayed on its moneys, and the unremitting care taken to give the readings of the inscriptions correctly, may be a sufficient security for this; and our critic, for want of any justifiable case to go upon, is driven to the grossest misrepresentations.

As to the inscription KERATI, on a coin of Caractacus, I think the legend is much better in that form, than the reading adopted by Mr. Akerman, and, I believe, generally by the whole of the Numismatic Society thirteen

years ago, when the coin was first discovered of MEPATI.
That reading, however, had an undisturbed currency for
a year or two, and an eminent popular writer, whose
works have gone through about twenty-five editions, wrote
a poem of some thirty stanzas on this supposed Mepati,
viewing him as a British prince of antiquity, and the
striker of the coin. (See the *Numismatic Chronicle* for July
1848, pp. 92-97), on the then explanation and attribution
of the coin. No one thought that the inscription was in
the Greek characters; but afterwards observing that some
other coins supposed to apply to Caractacus had an inter-
mixture of Greek letters in their legends, and that the
first letter was much more like a K than an M, I ventured,
notwithstanding the previous adverse dictum of high
authorities, to attribute the coin to Caractacus, which I
believe is its correct destination.

The critic asks (*Literary Gazette*, p. 320, col. 3, and
*Athenæum*, p. 441, col. 2), why the lettering should be in
Greek characters? The answer is, because Caractacus
was at war for nine years with the Romans (see the *Annals*
of Tacitus, xii, 36), and it is usual, when nations are at
war with each other, to discountenance and to forbid the
literature of the other side. Thus Alexander, the Emperor of Russia, discountenanced the teaching and speaking of the French language during the great French war
which he carried on with Napoleon I.

As to what he says (*Athenæum*, p. 441, col. 2) about
there not being representations of cases of sacrificial knives,
serpents, Druidical circles, and *bucrania*, *i. e.* skulls of
oxen which had been offered in sacrifice (see *Celt. Ins.*, pl.
i, fig. 6, and the other coins of that plate) on the coins
assigned to the sons of Cunobeline, I scarcely know what
he means. Mr. Akerman, as is sufficiently known, acknowledged that Druidical circles do appear on ancient
British coins (see *Numismatic Journal*, vol. i, p. 217), and I
have never seen them plainer delineated than on the
said coins, in some instances. *Bucrania* have been acknowledged to be on these coins by Mr. Birch. Serpents occur on the Roman imperial series of Africa as
well as on the coins here mentioned. Sacrificial knives
appear on the Roman altar found formerly at Whitehaven,
and inscribed VOLANTI VIVAS, and on other altars. The

cases of sacrificial knives were nearly triangular, and the three handles appear on one and the same side, which is exactly the case here (*Celt. Ins.*, pl. i, fig. 1). Therefore these objects, which are nearly as broad as they are long, cannot be swords, as some, for want of a better solution, have imagined.

I have expressed myself as follows in the passage which he has remarked upon : " The coins of Adminius and Togodumnus are noticeable from the occurrence of various symbols upon them, as bucrania, *i. e.* skulls of oxen, circles of dots, cases of sacrificial knives, double circles, serpents and loose horses. The upholding the nationality of the Britons and of the Druidical religion is supposed to be implied in these emblems" (*Celt. Insc.*, p. 38). In further remark, therefore, I just say that the loose horse is the most natural emblem of liberty; and the bucrania, Druidical circles, and sacrificial knives, indicate that they had their own religious rites; and as to the point of fact that the Druids did sacrifice animals, a deep trench some twenty feet long, filled with the skulls and other bones of the now extinct *bos longifrons* in the neighbourhood of Druidical remains near Kits Coty house, Kent, which was dug into and explored about the year 1844, abundantly testifies. Some of the bones were preserved in the Maidstone Museum.

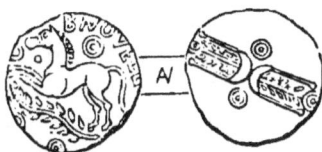

There are, however, a type or two of Dubnovellaunos, and indeed of Adminius, without most of the emblems here spoken of, that is, the serpent, the cases of sacrificial knives, and the *bucrania*, as in the instance which is here given.

To recur to the topic of the identity of Togodumnus and Dubnovellaunos. It seems difficult to imagine why there should have ever been any hesitation in admitting it. I conclude it could have only been, that it was preferred to bring forward the supposed new name of a British prince, rather than to identify an old one.

I will further say, with respect to the class of coins now referred to, that I think there is nothing that should meet with a warmer approval of numismatists than assigning certain types to the sons of Cunobeline. The coins are perfectly authentic, and specimens of them for the most part are to be seen in the British Museum; while various of them are engraved in the *Numismatic Journal*, vol. i, British coins, figs. 3, 4, 5, 6, 7, 8, and in the *Numismatic Chronicle* for July 1851, in the plate at p. 71, figs. 1, 3, 4, 5, 6, 9, 10.

There is thus a wide and unnatural chasm filled up in ancient British numismatics, for which, indeed, no real reason existed, though Dr. Pegge, in his *Coins of Cunobeline*, p. 20, declares that he could suggest nothing in his time to supply the blank. We are now able to present an authentic series of British kings for this particular epoch, and to go side by side with the accounts in Dion Cassius, Tacitus, and Suetonius.

The delineations on the coin which I have just given, and which is in gold, are: a loose horse on the obverse, and two crescents, ornamented, placed back to back on the reverse. The two brothers, Caractacus and Togo-dumnus, which last is Dubnovellaunos, we find, according to *Dion Cassius*, were both in the field together in the command of separate and distinct armies struggling for the liberties of their country against the Romans in the invasion of Aulus Plautius. Accordingly, the two crescents of the reverse on this coin of Dubnovellaunos so knit together may be significant—as we may judge—of the union, unfortunate as it turned out, between these two persons. The two crescents, similarly placed, occur on two or three other coins of much the same execution, as in Ruding's *Annals of the Coinage*, pl. ii, figs. 41, 42, and *Numismatic Chronicle* for July 1851, plate at p. 79, fig. 2.

As to another point touched upon in the *Literary Gazette*, p. 320, col. 2. The subject of the complete and altogether undeniable identity of the Punic, or rather Phœnician speeches in the *Pœnulus* of Plautus with the modern Irish, otherwise Gaelic, is one of the highest importance as regards the science of languages, ethnology, and the illustration of the Holy Scriptures. When the discovery, then, was made, which took the world by surprise, it was one of the most noted epochs of literature, and formed a sure basis for illustrating and knowing correctly the language of one of the four or five principal races of mankind ; but to a person like our critic, who has scarcely, as it would appear, read a line on the subject, and thought on it still less, it is of course a mere dead letter.

Respecting what he says (*Athenæum*, p. 441, col. 1) that I put forward a coin reading on the obverse PRASVTAGVS REX, &c., and on the other side IMPERATOR, I must, in answer to this, give this statement a flat contradiction, as I have no such coin in the whole volume.

The point, however, at which the critic aims, though he makes a false quotation, is, that it is contrary to numismatic rules that the word REX, which is a Celtic word as well as a Latin one, and implies " king," should appear on one side of a coin, and the word TASCIOVANVS, that is, military commander, on the other, as it does on one of the types of Cunobeline. Here again he shows himself entirely ignorant of the genius of the Celtic national coinage, as indeed he has only too often done before. But I need not say " Celtic coinage," for the same style is admissible in the coinage of any nation. For instance : Should a medallion be struck of the royal duke who now is at the head of the military forces of this country, how natural it would be to have his name, bust, and titles on one face of the coin, and the words COMMANDER IN CHIEF on the other. It is, then, truly extraordinary that any cavil should be made, or objections raised on this head.

But what a contrast does not our critic present! He assumes an overbearing and pretentious tone, as I have before observed, when he is dilating on his round of common-place topics, but his capabilities appear but of small dimensions when he is bringing forward any numismatic material of his own. For instance, see a proof of this in

what he says of the two British coins inscribed AMMINVS

and QVANGETH, which may be regarded as the two gems of
the ancient British coinage. The first is spoken of with
commendation by M. De la Saussaye in the *Revue Numismatique* for May and June 1847. It is, he says, "d'une
très jolie fabrique;" and the interpretation and attribution of it are due to the celebrated Marquis de Lagoy,
now deceased. The second was brought forward by the
late Mr. Beesley, the historian of Banbury, and, as it was
not long before his death, may be regarded as a legacy
from him to his country.

Now, were our critic really as much versed as he ought
to be in ancient British numismatics before taking upon
himself to disparage other explorers in the same path, he
certainly would do honour to the discovery of so eminent
a man in his own line of research as the Marquis de
Lagoy; instead of which he passes it by in a most con-
temptuous manner (*Literary Gazette*, p. 320, col. 3, and
*Athenæum*, p. 441, col. 2), and he professes not to be able
to see what a coin inscribed AMMINVS can have to do with
a British prince named Adminius!! The one is perhaps
not near enough in orthography to the other, he may be
disposed to think!!! As to the second coin, he is so un-
informed as a numismatist, that he evidently knows not
that it exists. He thinks that there must be some mistake about it; that it must be an invention, and that the
letters are only hoofs of horses and wheels of chariots, &c.
A brief account, therefore, of the bringing forward of this
very remarkable and most interesting coin is necessary,
and may accordingly here follow.

The gold coin inscribed QVANΓEƟ, that is, QVANGETH,
will be found described and classified, with a date also
assigned to it, in the *Coins of Cunobeline and the Ancient
Britons*, pp. 37-39, 63, and 281-285, and in the *Celtic
Inscriptions*, pp. 15, 35, and pl. ix, fig. 2. It was exhi-
bited by Mr. Alfred Beesley to the Numismatic Society,
December 22, 1842, as reported in their Proceedings for
that year, p. 88, where it would seem the legend was
given by some error as OVANTEO. This the rather appears,
as the *Gentleman's Magazine* for Jan. 1843, p. 78, in report-
ing the meeting of that evening, acquaints us, that the
reading of the legend was QVANTEO. A letter also from
a correspondent signing himself P in the succeeding July

number, p. 39, confirms the reading then given of QVANTEO. The T, however, being exactly in the form of an inverted L, makes the reading QVANGEO, and the final letter being not an O, but in reality a barred D, that is ө, which has the power of th or s, makes ultimately the reading QVANGEө, *i. e.* QVANGETH.

As far as my recollection extends, no engraving of the coin was inserted in the *Numismatic Chronicle.* Indeed I believe that Mr. Beesley sent no descriptive article of it; nor was it easy in the then confused and unclassified state of the ancient British coinage, further than describing the delineations of the obverse and reverse, and reciting the legend, to give any very definite account of it. Another gentleman also, named Hobson, had a gold coin either of the same type or one very similar, and I had the opportunity of seeing either Mr. Hobson's or Mr. Beesley's coin, then in the hands of a friend, in the course of the year 1844.

My first actual "to do" with the coin QVANGETH was in the year 1848, when, writing to Mr. Beesley for wax impressions, he very politely forwarded me them, and not long afterwards, though too late to be used for engraving, forwarded also an electrotype. I subjoin a copy of his letter sent to me at the same time as the impressions.

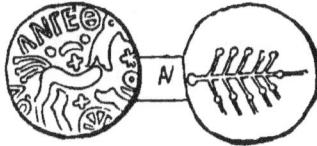

"SIR,—Agreeably to your wish I forward an impression of my gold British coin. It was found in 1842 in a field near Bourton, and two miles north of Banbury. The weight is 82 grains. You will observe that the concave, or obverse side (reversed by the wax into the convex one) has the rude figure of a horse, with other devices, and the letters QVANГEө. Antiquaries have read these (letters) OVANTEө, QVANGETH, QVANGEO, and QVANTEO. I suppose the reverse is a fern leaf. My own fancy is that the coin is the work of a rude British artist, who did not know what letters he was imitating. Owing to the shape of

D

the coin, and the wretchedness of modern wax, I have been obliged to substitute a sulphur impression.

" I shall be obliged by your sending me an impression of the woodcut as soon as your artist has done one. Perhaps it would not be amiss if, as soon as he gets an early proof, he were to send it me to compare (it) with the coin before you go to press with it, as there may be parts more distinct on the coin than on the wax impression.                 I am, Sir,
                                  " Yours obediently,
"Banbury, Feb. 16, 1848.            ALFRED BEESLEY."

Mr. Beesley's letter will be useful in giving us an account of the casual ideas of numismatists and antiquaries soon after it was found, of the probable orthography of the coin, till it settled down to its present reading of QVANGETH. It also shows the preliminaries for engraving the coin, as in pl. ix, 2, which was most faithfully done by Mr. Fairholt.

Now our critic having with great absurdity, but only with his usual rashness otherwise, asserted that the first two letters of the legend QVANGETH are only hoofs of horses or wheels of chariots (*Literary Gazette*, p. 320, col. 3, and *Athenæum*, p, 441, col. 2); in consequence of this I lately submitted Mr. Beesley's sulphur casts and his wax impressions to two of the most eminent numismatists in London, whose names could be mentioned, and who pronounced the imputation entirely groundless, the letters being remarkably distinct, and quite clear and separate from the legs of the horse delineated on the coin. I also showed the sulphur cast and impressions to an eminent numismatic friend in the country, whose judgment appeared likewise fully to coincide.

I will here just observe that this type of Mr. Beesley's is not the same as the British Museum specimen, which has not the Q; nor is it the same, as once supposed, as the two coins engraved in Dr. Wise's plate of British coins, plate xvi, p. 281, figs. 3 and 6, in his *Bodleian Catalogue*, folio, 1750, which also have not the Q.

Our coin inscribed QVANGEӨ, or *Quangeth*, is evidently tantamount to Quanges, *i. e.* the Canges, or Cangi, who occupied the present Staffordshire and Warwickshire. The name of this ancient British tribe is mentioned by Tacitus in his *Annals*, xii, 32, and also occurs on pigs of lead in the form " Kiangi." Regarding the "eth" or "es" being substituted for the "i," the same thing often occurs in ancient names, which are frequently so varied in their terminations on coins; though in classical or modern authors they may have a fixed orthography. As Eduis (Edues) see *Lelewel*, pl. vii, fig. 9, for Ædui and ECES, *i. e.* EC(EN)ES, for the Iceni of Tacitus. See our *Celtic Inscriptions*, pl. iii. 1. This coin, then, applies to the Cangi, an ancient state in Britain; and we have the very parallel instance to it in the Gaulish coinage, both in the form of the word and the unusual character introduced into its orthography as VELIOCAΘI (see *Lelewel*, pl. vii, fig. 5) for the Veliocasses, who were a people of Armorica.

Our coin QVANGETH has another characteristic, for it is one of a class which has a singular ornament on the reverse, which is most commonly called the "fish bone" ornament, from some little resemblance, though not an entire resemblance, to the back-bone of a fish (see *Celtic Inscriptions*, plate ix, 2). This class of coins, with the fish-bone ornament, as I may here subjoin, did not belong to any one single state, since we have their legends, CATTI, CORI, QVANGETH, COMVX (*i. e.* COMMIOS, VXACONA), BODVOC (one type), and lastly RIGVANTES, *i. e. Regentes*, see *Ravennas*. They appear rather to have been states under a league and confederacy; and the names, I feel a full persuasion, apply to the various states acting in unison with Caractacus during his nine years war with the Romans, and adopting the principle of independency (see Tacitus, *Annals*, xii, 36). Our critic, it seems, did not recollect, at the time he indited his remarks, the five other varying inscriptions, and so made the great mistake of supposing that the coin, QVANGETH, was the same as another of the fish-bone class belonging to quite a different state, the Riguantes or Regentes (see *Literary Gazette*, p. 320, col. 3, and *Athenæum*, p. 441, col. 2), to which I shall now advert.

He affirms, with great gravity, that the legend, QVANGEΘ, or QVANGETH, in reality, reads ANTED, and is part of a supposed reading, ANTEDRIGV (see *Literary Gazette*, p. 320, *loco citato*; and he says in the *Athenæum*,

in the passage I have above referred to, with surprising
coolness, that I seem quite unaware that the legends on
this (coin, *i. c.* QVANGETH) and similar specimens, are
written shortly, ANTED, and in fuller and more perfect
specimens, ANTEDRIGV. In answer, I am not indeed
aware of the circumstance, simply from the reason, that a
coin, with the legend he mentions, has never yet been
struck, either by the ancient or modern Britons ; and,
what is more, never will be struck ; unless some forger,
compassionating a case of distress, should manufacture one
for our critic's use, and pass it off upon him as a genuine
coin.   It is indeed surprising that any one at all versed
in numismatical studies should not be able to read so
easy a coin inscription as that of RIGVANTES.   The cause,
however, of his mistake is this : the legend RIGVANTES is
inscribed in two main portions on the opposite sides of
the obverse or face of the coin ; RIG stands by itself, then
a wide space intervenes, after which the letter V occurs
by itself ; then another wide space, and lastly comes the
concluding portion ANTETH.   That is the form in which
it is inserted, and it is admitted that it reads from right
to left ; so we have duly and properly RIGVANTES.   Our
critic, unluckily for himself, begins at the latter half of
the word, puts the cart before the horse, and so obtains
the preposterous reading of ANTEDRIGV.

The Riguantes or Regentes, mentioned by Ravennas,
in the work called his *Chorography*, and by no other
author, must have been one of the principal divisions or
states of the Southern Belgæ of Britain ; possibly the
main tribe : *i. e.* those that occupied Hampshire and
Wiltshire.

He makes the assertion that ANTED frequently appears
by itself, on the obverses of these types (see as above),
it does so ; and when that is the case, it may reasonably
be concluded that the rim may be deficient on the opposite corresponding side of the obverse, or some other
cause prevents the appearance of the first syllable, RIG.
It is indeed somewhat singular how often the word ANTES,
which, I suppose, in the Celtic language of those times
meant " people," stands alone on the coins of the Iceni.
See *Celtic Inscriptions*, pl. iii, figs. 4, 5, and 6, where it is
expressed in monogram ; but I have only one instance,

pl. ix, fig. 5, and as shown in the next page, where the
IIVG, the first syllable of the word IVGANTES, presents
itself to view.

The readers of these pages will, perhaps, excuse my
having gone into the subject of the coin inscribed
QVANGETH, with so much circumstantial detail. It is
done because the critic makes it one of the principal
points of attack ; and puts it forth as his main criterion
as to whether the work on *Celtic Inscriptions* can be
depended on as an authority. I think, in the result, that
this, his most unskilful attempt, will only rebound upon
himself to his own detriment, and supply a most obvious
and convincing proof of his own incapacity.

The coins of the Iceni, to which the type QVANGETH
belongs, certainly form a most important portion of the
ancient British coinage, and, in many respects, supply an
example of a coinage, *per se*, which varies much from that
of Cunobeline. There is one very remarkable feature,
which I should not omit to mention. The Iceni introduced very numerous monograms on their coins, and
have other modes, almost peculiar to. themselves, of
expressing their legends ; for the shank bones of horses
often form parts of letters in their delineations of types,
as can be seen in numerous instances in the coins of the
Iceni, as preserved in the British Museum, and in engravings in the *Numismatic Chronicle*. See also *Celtic
Inscriptions*, pl. iii, figs. 2, 3, 4, 5, and 6, where there are
several coins which are thus noticeable, faithfully represented. Likewise there are further instances in. the
British Museum ; see also figs. 1, 3, 6, on the same plate,
where a loose bridle is delineated, to form a species of
long s, at the conclusion of the word ECE(NE)s. The
critic must know all this well enough, if he has any pre-
tensions of being acquainted with ancient British coins ;
and if he does not know these things, how can he suppose
himself qualified to assume the position of an arbitrator
or judge in these discussions! Whether the types of

Caractacus, inscribed KERAT and KERATI, in Greek letters, which indeed belong to another state, namely, to the Southern Belgæ, and not to the Iceni, come under this category of fanciful representation, I do not know. I have given the coins faithfully as they are; and the point is, in fact, of no consequence to me; for I am not answerable as to how particular tribes of the Celts chose to configurate the letters of their legends, whether absurdly or not, any more that Sir Henry Rawlinson is for the Assyrians conjoining mens' heads to the bodies of bulls or lions; or than Sir Gardner Wilkinson is for the Egyptians putting hawks' heads on human shoulders. I am only answerable as supplying correct copies of legends, and representations of how they are formed.

Nevertheless, I must not be understood as admitting, which I do not, that the letters of the legend referred to are formed in the fanciful way in which the critic appears to suppose they are. I leave that an open question. However, from a comparison with the Icenian legends, I am certain that in either case, the readings of the two coins respectively, KERAT and KERATI, were intended.

I may here mention, that what is called the fish-bone on the reverses of various coins which have been alluded to, and supposed to have been struck during the wars of Caractacus, is evidently not a fish-bone, as it has been styled for want of a better term to describe it; nor is it a fern leaf, which it is not in the least like, and still less a bearded ear of corn, to both which last objects some have assigned it.

Almost the most that can be done is accurately to describe this emblem, which, strange to say, has not been done hitherto.

Imprimis, it had a straight stem or staff, at the bottom of which is invariably a pommel or round knob. Ten spikes are inserted into this stem, at about an angle of seventy-five degrees, all in the same plane and issuing from it exactly opposite to each other. There are twelve spikes in some specimens. Each of these spikes appears to pass through a ball for about a third of its length, as we gather from Mr. Beesley's coin, see our page 17 *ante*, which supplies the most perfect pattern of this object known. In that specimen, all the spikes on both sides, in reality, pass through the balls, though the engraving only represents those on one side to do so. The stem also ends in a spike at its extremity, which likewise appears to have its ball inserted upon it, though passed much further down upon it than the others, as in Mr. Beesley's specimen. The emblem thus formed of a common stem, balls, and branches, and which occurs in no other known coinage but the ancient British, might have been transmitted from tribe to tribe, as occasion required, as a summons for a general gathering; as the " shupatties" were in the Indian rebellion of 1857, or as the " brand " is described to have been, in the poem of the *Lady of the Lake*. The Gauls, as we are informed by Tacitus, *Histories*, i, 54, in speaking of the Lingones, a state of that country, were accustomed to send round representations of right hands, when they made a league or expressed their friendship. His words are, "Miserat civitas Lingonum vetere instituto dona legionibus, dextras hospitii insignia." In English, " The state of the Lingones had sent according to their old custom, gifts to the legions and effigies of 'right hands,' which were considered as the 'insignia' of cordiality." See *Lelewel*, p. 135, and *Lambert*, p. 85. These representations of hands appear frequently on their coins.

I possess no materials to be able to acquaint the reader with the precise ideas which were associated by the ancient Britons with this emblem in its various details; though I feel much confidence that I am correct as to my ideas of its general use, as stated above.

I should not here omit a circumstance much connected with the subject of a shortly preceding page. It was about twelve years ago, when, wishing to ascertain more correctly a legend of the Iceni, for I then read the two most obvious ones, as ECES and ATA (see the *Coins of Cunobeline*, p. 95), I applied to my friend, Mr. C. Roach Smith, whose assistance is usually very effective on most topics. The occasion in question was no exception, and making out a hasty sketch on a scrap of paper, torn from the enclosure of some articles which had been forwarded to him, he showed at once how the Icenian monogram, ATD, should be expanded into a much longer form ; his sketch also showed the fanciful custom of this ancient British state, to which I have before alluded, of forming occasionally a letter, as it suited them, from a portion of the horse. I have accordingly inserted here a woodcut of the origi-nal diagram, with which he favoured me, which in its full reading is ANTED, *i. e.* ANTES ; Mr. C. Roach Smith's specimen, it seems, not giving the cross-bar of the D, or the middle and lower strokes of the E impressed on other types of Icenian coins. I can now only hope that the critic, if he does not believe me, will believe Mr. C. Roach Smith—and so I leave the matter.

Another thing is noticeable, and forms a prominent feature in these proceedings ; which is, that from some new move, from some precious contrivance, and from the impatience of some one to annihilate a victim, two attacks appear on the same day, the same 5th of October, and are inserted in two very influential and important Journals, among those which guide public opinion, namely the *Lite-rary Gazette* and *Athenæum*. However, as the attacks are such as admit of an answer, this proves in the end rather a benefit than otherwise; as I am thus enabled to reply to them both together.

Regarding his mention of Julius Cæsar and Philip II of Macedonia, in the *Literary Gazette* and *Athenæum :* respecting the first, I hold the opinion of those numis-matists, generally considered the most judicious, who maintain that what are called the consular and family coins, were not struck till the sway of Julius Cæsar com-menced ; as to the second, I confine myself strictly to the Greek coinage ; and if there be a few trifling exceptions, the critic must have the advantage of them. However, these points are altogether extraneous to the present subject.

I have thus answered the main objections of the critic, many of which would certainly never have been advanced, if he had not been *under par* in his knowledge of the ancient Celtic coinages of Gaul and Britain; for instance, among others, the objection respecting the titular form of the names of the Gaulish chiefs in the Gaulish coinage, and the cavils about the legend, QVANGETH, in the British coinage. These would never have been made, had he known the real facts in either case. His observations, I must add, are written in the most acrimonious style that can be conceived. But what I most complain of, is the narrow-minded spirit in which they are indited. For instance, contrary to the usual custom, he gives scarcely a third of the title, and conceals that the work contains a Glossary, and Atlas of Coins. That, of course, is done from a most unhandsome and illiberal feeling. I can only ask the critic how he can reconcile his attack on the work with the knowledge which he must have engraven in his own mind, that in it, and in the *Coins of Cunobeline and of the Ancient Britons*, classification has been first supplied to the ancient British coinage; which has been reduced into form and arrangement, from a state, as he knows, of the utmost disorder; and he must be well aware that all future writers, and he himself among the rest, must follow this classification; for it would indeed be absurd to assign, at the present day, the coins of the Iceni to the Southern Belgæ of Britain, or those of either to the Brigantes; or those of the sons of Cunobeline to that monarch. Regardless, however, of all considerations, he makes his attacks with misrepresentations the most gross, and is chargeable with levity as well as ill-will; for a great part of his objections are merely captious, and have no basis of any argument to support them.

In recapitulation: the work of the *Celtic Inscriptions* has been published as a collection of facts to illustrate the state of ancient Britain in the century before the Christian era, and the first century afterwards; and it is intended to be a work of reference and authority as supplying materials for the early history of this country. This being the case, and the work being attacked by a person incompetent in ancient British numismatics; or by the same person and a confederate, in two of the most leading and influential journals that are in circulation, on the same day, who takes upon him to assert that the readings of the inscriptions on the coins are made with no skill (see the *Literary Gazette*, pp. 319, col. 3, and 320, col. 3; and the *Athenæum*, p. 441, col. 2), and that the publication, as a work of reference, is of no authority (see the *Literary Gazette*, p. 319, col. 3, and p. 320, col. 2, and *Athenæum*, p. 440, col. 3, *et alibi*), besides other disparaging remarks. This being the case, I have not hesitated, and I suppose the same course would be taken by most others,

E

to draw up an answer to his aspersions, both on my own account and that of my publisher, and also that of my readers, who have a right to have such imputations cleared up; accordingly I here give a plain and direct contradiction to his most unwarrantable statements.

The critic, in reality, from his ignorance and misapprehension, would throw back the whole ancient British coinage into the most perfect chaos and confusion, now that it is only just emerging from it. The reader, therefore, will be glad, with every true numismatist, that I have been able, as before noted, to overthrow his main position, and to prove that the names of the Gaulish chiefs, as inserted on the ancient moneys of that country, are titular; a fact which he scoffed at exceedingly, and pronounced to be my invention. In losing this point, he must himself see that his chief stronghold is gone; for by this it becomes evident that the titular principle of interpreting Celtic coinages is introduced, and must be followed, and carried out. This brings him to the same system and path in which I have proceeded myself, and which every dispassionate inquirer must adopt. He must now perceive that ancient British numismatics are not a subject on which off-hand opinions can be hazarded; but that they must be treated step by step with due caution. His other objections, which are very various in their scope and object, and which are somewhat numerous, I think I have answered satisfactorily; though my present space is too circumscribed to refer to them again in detail.

His second leading, and most important point, is certainly the position he takes up about the coin QVANGETH, a coin which the critic has evidently never seen. In regard to this coin, as before noted, the testimony has been given me of three of the first numismatists in the kingdom, and I could have, I have no doubt, the testimony of the whole Numismatic Society, that every letter of the legend is on the coin, and fully clear from the hoofs, or any other part of the horse, or anything else on this piece of money. His second stronghold is thus gone: and what are we to think of a numismatist affecting to be an adept in the ancient British series being unacquainted with this fine and truly characteristic specimen of these

moneys.  Nearly as much might be said of his rejection
of another fine coin inscribed AMMINVS, in the classical
style of representation, which is frequently adopted in
these moneys, as well as the rude Celtic types.  This
coin, which is of the highest interest, was duly read and
appropriated by the Marquis de Lagoy some years ago.

In conclusion, I have only to remind the reader, that
the ancient British coinage having been much disparaged
and but little regarded as to its historical and documental
value, as supplying materials for the early history of our
island, I have endeavoured to set it forth in its due pro-
minency and relief in the *Celtic Inscriptions*, the statements of which it has been my purpose to vindicate in
these few pages.

I have endeavoured to assert nothing that is not fully
substantiated; but I have been treated with the most
inconsiderate injustice in doing so, and indeed in the
most uncandid way.  But as the materials are of value to
illustrate the early state of the island, and to go side by
side with the accounts of classic authors who mention
Britain, I should not be justified had I omitted them.

The attack which has been made upon me has been, on
my part, quite unprovoked.  I have given no just cause
of offence to any one.  I have sought no contest with anyone; but being assailed, I have shown the groundless
nature of the misrepresentations which have been brought
forward against me.

There will be necessarily one effect produced by these
discussions, namely, that they will tend to make all
persons more acquainted with the subject of our early
British coinage, by which many of the ancient Celtic
states of the island, almost entirely forgotten, are brought
again into notice: the positions, indeed, of which were
only shown before, by a few old maps.  But now a line of
ancient Celtic kings is held up to our view who once
figured away as ruling the destinies of this or that portion
of the island, and issued their coinage.  We may enume-
rate Cunobeline as the first of these, whose father, Timancius, is mentioned in the celebrated inscription at Ancyra,
in Asia Minor, recording the Acts of Augustus, and who
made treaties with that emperor (see Strabo's *Geography*,
book iv), and occupied the attention of the Roman poets,

Propertius and Horace. This sovereign, it seems, had his own naval forces to protect our shores, which acted against the Roman provincial naval armaments of Gaul (see Propertius, *Elegies*, ii, 20, 68, and *Celtic Inscriptions*, pp. 119-121). Cunobeline had a copious coinage, we know; and his two sons, Adminius and Togodumnus, for the time they reigned—which was some three or four years, or more—are now first shown to have had quite their proportionable share; for these two seem altogether to have displayed the coining propensities of their father: though we have only a few specimens of the moneys of Caractacus, another son, who reigned nine years in his own right (see Tacitus, *Annals*, xii, 36), his attention being probably too much otherwise engaged: while a fourth son, Belinus (*Triad*, 79), for some reason, did not coin at all. We have, besides, the coinage of Prasutagus, king of the Iceni, mentioned by Tacitus (*Annals*, xiv, 31), and the coinage of Bericus or Vericus, mentioned by Suetonius and Dion Cassius, who appears to have been an ally of the Romans, but otherwise a species of nondescript person, except that he was a king or chief of the Southern Belgæ or Firbolgi of Britain towards the middle of the first century. We have likewise the coinage of Eppillus, whom there is good reason for supposing to have been the Carvillius of Julius Cæsar, another king of the Southern Belgæ whose dominions appear to have been in Kent (see his *Commentaries, Gaulish Wars*, v, 18). In short, there is not, to my knowledge, any ancient British coinage except of persons whose names are mentioned in history, and except of one or two chiefs whose existence seems to be implied, as VIR. REX, *i. e.*, king or ruler at Viridunum; but there is scarcely another instance: as I am fully persuaded, that the two coins inscribed REX CALLE in the British Museum (see Mr. Akerman's *Coins of Cities and Princes*, pl. xxi, figs. 8 and 9) are moneys of Caractacus, they having a portion of his name, (K)ERR(ATIK), inscribed on their reverses in Greek letters. This remark may perhaps be of considerable use for guidance of other numismatists and researchers, for there seems the greatest probability that as to other new types which may hereafter come to light, that they will be found to belong to some classes of British moneys already known. Coins of some of the minor states of the Iceni, unmentioned before, may be found; but scarcely can there be expected that new names of princes or rulers will appear, except perhaps in the quarter of the Southern Belgæ, just mentioned, where it is very feasible that further titular names of chiefs may be discovered somewhat after the form of VIR. REX, which has been before alluded to. Some of the successors of Eppillus in those regions may very possibly have issued their types; otherwise, as the Celtic coinage, except perhaps some few types of the Brigantes, ceased generally in Britain, about the year 62, by the conquest of the Iceni, it is very improbable that the insurgents, either in the time of Domitian or Arviragus, mentioned by Juvenal, or those in the time of Hadrian or Antoninus, were sufficiently established in their power to think of reviving the monetary issues of their predecessors. We have no Pixtilus in the ancient British coinage the same as there was in Gaul, an indefinite personage of whom little is known, but who struck a rather profuse coinage, and not in such very bad taste.

I may suggest, and the thing indeed is but too evident, that the progress of ancient British numismatical science has been much checked by erroneous application and assignment of various types of our Celtic coins. It may be seen with regret that our numismatists, who have of late years discovered new types of British coins, have not been so fortunate in duly applying their discoveries. Relative to which point I have endeavoured to show that Mr. Birch's discovery of new types of Dubnovellaunos is in reality applicable to Togodumnus; as also that Mr. Evans' discovery of the coins of Aededomaros actually applies to Adminius, and his later discovery, though read very otherwise by him, to the Riguantes or Regentes mentioned by Ravennas in his *Chorography*. The advance made by the three discoveries duly assigned is considerable.

In retrospect of the present vindication of the *Celtic Inscriptions* which I have considered incumbent on me to make, I find it has had the effect of passing before us in review a great many of the principal points of the ancient British coinage, and somewhat prominently so. Discussion, indeed, is a great awakener of attention; for an historical point, first asserted, then questioned, re-asserted and canvassed in all its features, is assuredly fixed more on the mind than if it were laid down merely as a simple matter of fact, and not referred to afterwards.

I have had engraved for the present *Vindication*, as the reader will observe, a plate of facsimiles from Pompeii. The forms of the R are curious; and it will be readily no-ticed that some of the rarer configurations of the letters, as those of the E and P, occur on Gaulish and British coins. A close comparison would doubtlessly detect some others. At the same time, both the said coinages, on their part, have several letters of rare forms of which there is no trace whatever in the Inscriptions at Pompeii.    It is possible that the form of the R as in the plate may have been, or may be, the cause of false readings; as, for instance, of the L for R in the word FIR.   Numismatists will therefore thank me for putting them on their guard. I have collected the fac-similes of the letters from the learned and interesting work of Dr. Christopher Words-worth, his *Inscriptions of Pompeii*, published in 1838. The only fault of his work is that it is too short.    The paging, it may be necessary to say, given in the plate is that which refers to his publication.

I also add a list of the legends as in the plates of the *Celtic Inscriptions*, and a brief summary of the extent and general contents of the ancient British coinage.

## ADDENDA.

SINCE inditing the foregoing few pages, an article has come to hand containing various further remarks on the *Celtic Inscriptions*, inserted in the *Numismatic Chronicle*, for December 1861, vol. i, new series, pp. 248-9.   This is written somewhat more moderate in tone than the former two in the *Literary Gazette* and *Athenæum*, and without the same coarse invective; but is distinguished by the same taint of misrepresentation, as I had almost said there is a misrepresentation in every line; however, there are certainly several, in the aggregate, in every paragraph. This may happen from carelessness.   Otherwise we may judge of the pitiable state of a writer who should be driven to such expedients, and who should act thus from thinking that the majority of his readers would not compare his remarks with the original, and so find out the deception.

With regard to titular names : the writer of the article makes some observations generally as to the origin of names, which, as far as present inquiries are concerned, are perfectly superfluous. The question here merely is as to the matter of fact; whether titular names were, or were not, extensively in use during the Gaulish and British coining periods. I have proved that they were, and the writer of the article has nothing else to do except to show the contrary, on which point he has not said a single word. .

As to the somewhat multiplied names of various British chiefs, the writer disingenuously conceals the explanation given, that the names which are mostly titular, applied to distinct periods of time in the lifetimes of those who bore them, to different commands they had, and to different provinces over which they presided. Our own Prince of Wales, were he to coin after the old Celtic fashion, would be found to have several *aliases*. As Duke of Cornwall, Duke of Lancaster, Prince of Wales, etc., etc., etc. So this matter is sufficiently answered.

However, the shafts in this new semi-attack are by far too ill-directed, and projected with too little force to require a specific answer. The attempt to travestie the legend, vvicv, first engraved in Gibson's *Camden*, and from him copied by Dr. Pegge, in his *Coins of Cunobeline*, is merely absurd and not in the slightest degree, whatever, warranted by representations of the coin in either author ; nor ever suggested, I believe, on any former occasion when the coin has been referred to. Why did not the writer give the legend cvn, on the reverse of this coin ? Simply because, had he done so, it would have refuted, or at least very much weakened, his own argument; as he probably is numismatist enough to know that cvn does not occur on both faces of Cunobeline's coins, except in one instance, where it is supposed to stand on one side for the first syllable of the word *Cunetio*. Also he must be conscious that when any portion of the

name of Cunobeline occurs on one face of a coin, it is the
name of a place which must be expected to be found on
the other, as in the present instance:—obverse, CVN:
reverse, VVICV, *i. e.*, apparently " Huiccum."

With respect to the Atlas of coins which the writer of
the article mentions *en passant*, it may be as well to say a
few words as to what has been proposed to be accomplished
in it.

It has been endeavoured to be so arranged as to show
many of the principal features and classifications of the
ancient British coinage at one view. The reader may see
in it the general character of Cunobeline's coinage and
that of his sons, as contrasted with the collateral and
nearly contemporaneous coinages of the southern Belgæ
of Britain and of the Iceni. At the same time due
delineations are supplied of the very unartistic, though
national and characteristic, coinages of the Brigantes and
Dumnonii, who attempted, in their way, and it would
appear on the whole rather copiously so, to supply the
materials of a public monetary circulation.

The main anxiety of this writer comes in last, which
is to shake, if possible, the credit of the Icenian coin,
VRE(IS) BOD . TASCIA. I happened to know of this coin
from nearly the very first; and I understand that it was
originally sold for twopence, or some such price, by the
person who found it—no great sum to tempt a forger.
It may be true that some few forged coins were met with
formerly in Suffolk; but there is not the slightest reason
to believe that the coin above referred to, was ever
originally regarded as such, or ever formed one of them.
Many genuine ancient British coins are discovered from
time to time in Suffolk, and we may view this as one of
the number; and consider it, as preserved, as an important historical document to the nation. This valuable
coin is in the possession of Mr. C. Roach Smith.

I may refer to the *Celtic Inscriptions*, p. 45, to show
that this coin is one of the decisive evidences of the true
meaning of the word " tasciovanus " or " tasciavanus."

In any case, it is scarcely doubtful that the first syllable
of the name Prasutagus was expressed in Roman British
times by the letters VRA or VRE.

DESCRIPTIVE LIST OF THE MONEYS OF ANCIENT
BRITISH STATES AND KINGS, AS ENGRAVED IN THE
ATLAS OF COINS, IN THE "CELTIC INSCRIPTIONS;"
*with their correct readings, and a portion of them with their
abbreviations filled up at full length.*

## PLATE I.

### COINS CHIEFLY OF THE SONS OF CUNOBELINE.

1. Adminius, legend AED(EDOMAROS); rev. no inscription
2. Adminius, legend AED(EDOMAROS); rev. no inscription
3. Togodumnus(DVBNOVELL)AVNOS, *semi retro.*; rev. blank
4. Togodumnus (DVBNOVELLA)VNOS, *semi-retro.*; rev. blank
5. Forgery producing legend CVNO. See *Celt.Ins.*, pp. 52-4
6. Coin with the legend TASCIAV ; rev. no inscription
7. Coin of Verulam, TASC ; reverse no inscription
8 Coin of the Southern Belgæ, inscribed CATTI

## PLATE II.

### COINS OF THE BRIGANTES.

1. Coin inscribed DVMNOCOVEPOS ; reverse VOS
2. Ditto DVMNOCOVEP ; reverse VOSILIOS
3. Ditto ASVP AS(VP) ; reverse none
4. Ditto VEP CORF; reverse none
5. Ditto TIGIION ; reverse VMI
6. Coin uninscribed
7. Ditto
8. Ditto

## PLATE III.

### COINS, CHIEFLY OF THE ICENI.

1. Coin inscribed EC(EN)ES ; reverse no inscription
2. Coin ditto ECEN(ES); reverse none
3. Coin ditto ELY, qu. ECE ? reverse none
4. Ditto ANTEƟ *i.e.* ANTETH, in monogram ; reverse none
5. Ditto ANTEƟ *i.e.* ANTETH or ANTES, in mon.; rev. none
6. Idem
7. Coin inscribed SITMV ; reverse none
8. Coin inscribed CORI ; reverse none
9. Dubnovellaunos DVRNAVNOS (misread ?); rev. none
10. Coin of the Iceni. Common also to Gaul

F

## PLATE IV.

### COINS OF THE DUMNONII.

1. Karnbré coin; type of Philip II of Macedonia
2. Idem
3. Karnbré coin
4. Idem and reverse with bird and boughs
5. Rude Karnbré coin
6. Karnbré coin ; type of Philip II
7. Ditto
8. Ditto

## PLATE V.

### VARIOUS COINS OF CUNOBELINE.

1. Coin, obverse CAM(VLODVNO); reverse CVN(OBELINI)
2. Obverse no inscription ; reverse TASCIO(VANI)
3. CVN(OBELINI) ; reverse none
4. Obverse CAMV ; reverse CVN retrograde
5. Obverse CVN(OBELINI); reverse CVN(ETIO) apparently
6. Obverse TASCIO(VANI) ; reverse CVNOBELI(NI)
7. CVNOBILIN(I); reverse CAM(VLODVNO)
8. Obverse none ; reverse SEGO(NTIO)
9. Obverse TASCIO(VANI); reverse SEGO(NTIO)
10. Obverse CVN(OBELINI); reverse SOLID(VN)O i.e. Bath
11. Obverse none; reverse TASCIO-RICON
12. Obverse CVNOBE(LINI); reverse TASC(IOVANI) FIR(BOLG)

## PLATE VI.

I. Various coins of the sons of Cunobeline
II. Various coins of the Southern Belgæ of Britain

1. Adminius, legend AMMINVS ; reverse DVN
2. Togodumnus (DV)BNOVELL(AVNOS); rev. no inscription
3. Caractacus, CEARATIC ; reverse TASCI F(IRBOLG)
4. Southern Belgic coin, EPPI. COM.; rev. no inscription
5. Coin of Eppillus, EPPI. COM.; reverse no legend
6. Coin of the Southern Belgæ, COM . F.; rev. illegible
7. Coin of Eppillus and Viridunum, CO . VIR ; reverse EPPI . COM . F.
8. Coin of Tincontium (Winchester), TIN ; reverse KOMF
9. Ditto, TIN ; reverse COM

## PLATE VII.

### COINS OF THE SOUTHERN BELGÆ CONTINUED.

1. Southern Belgic coin, inscription illegible
2. Ditto, uninscribed
3. Ditto, com .f.; reverse illegible
4. Coin of Vericus, (veri)cv(s); reverse (c)ommi
5. Coin, inscribed Catti, (k)att(i); reverse none. See *Celt. Insc.*, p. 125.
6. Coin of Tincontium, obverse cf; reverse tinc
7. Coin of Viridunum, obverse vir; reverse com.
8. Coin of Tincontium, obverse tin(contio); rev. none
9. Rom. coin countermarked, m. agri(ppa)cos. iii; rev. tin
10. Symbolical type of the Southern Belgæ, uninscribed and unexplained

## PLATE VIII.

i. Various coins of the Brigantes
ii. Miscellaneous coins

1. Coin of the Brigantes, dvmnocovep; rev. vosilios
2. Ditto, obverse vep; reverse obliterated
3. Ditto, no legend
4. Ditto, obverse corf; reverse no legend
5. Coin unclassed, found at Whaddon Chase, no legend
6. Ditto, ditto, ditto
7. Coin of the Dobuni, obverse bodvo(c); rev. none

## PLATE IX.

i. Various coins of the Iceni
ii. Coins to show the origin and progress of the Gaulish coinage

1. Coin of the Iceni uninscribed
2. Coin of the Cangi, qvangeth; reverse uninscribed
3. Coin of the Iceni, (e)cen(es); reverse no legend
4. Coin of the Iceni, obv. vre (retro.) bod; rev. tasci(a)
5. Iceni, cam(vlos) dvro(trigon); rev. iivg(antes)
6. Coin of Massilia, obverse no legend; reverse ma.
7. Macedonian stater of Philip II; reverse ΦIΛIΠΠOY
8. Gaulish imitation of ditto; reverse ΤIΛIIIΠOY
9. Another Gaulish imitation; reverse ini.

## PLATE X.

i. Gaulish coinage, continued
ii. Miscellaneous coins
iii. Specimens of forged and doubtful coins

1. Gaulish coin
2. Gaulish coin
3. Gaulish coin, with androcephalous horse
4. Coin of the Channel Islands
5. Coin, unclassed, legend, DIAS
6. Forged coin of Caractacus, CARIC, from coin of Carissa
7. Do. of Boadicea, BOADI, from coin of Apollo Musagetes
8. Do. of Arviragus, with the legend ARVI
9. Ditto ditto, with ARVI
10. Coin, inscribed ANDO

## PLATE XI.

i. Coins misread by early writers
ii. Fac-similes of legends
iii. The Marquis of Lagoy's types to illustrate British chariots

1. Coin read REX COM, to read VIR REX COMF
2. Coin read DIRETE, to read VIR REX
3. Fac-simile of legend, KERAT
4. Ditto, KERATI
5. Do., AEDIID (AEDED), part of the word AEDEDOMAROS
6. Ditto, AED
7. Ditto, TASC . FIR
8. Roman family coin, inscribed CAESAR IMP
9. Ditto ditto, inscribed L . HOSTILIVS SASERN(A)

---

The following few remarks on the plates may perhaps be useful.

PLATE I. will not only give a good idea of the types represented, but has the advantage of being taken from well preserved specimens; such, indeed, the coins of the sons of Cunobeline are usually found to be.

PLATE II. The coins in this plate, which are those of the Brigantes, are engraved from specimens in the British

Museum, or in the York Museum. The delineations on them seem to exhibit traces of a common though remote origin from the staters of Macedonia, but the legends are too obscure to admit of correct interpretation.

PLATE III. The first six of these coins, which are those of the Iceni, afford an instance of monograms or abbreviations in their legends beyond any others that are known. They are in that respect, as well as otherwise, of much interest. The coins in the plate are engraved from specimens in the British Museum collection, except figs. 7 and 10, which were from the cabinet of Mr. Huxtable.

PLATE IV. The portraits of the extensive find of coins called the Karnbré coins, appear to have been faithfully taken by Dr. Borlase in his *History of Cornwall*, folio 1750, and there only, it would seem, can any connected series of them be now found represented. The coins themselves, except figs. 1, 2, and 5, the latter very barbarous, it seems, are rather difficult to be met with. They were mostly, according to Dr. Borlase's representations, in a somewhat homely style of execution.

PLATE V will perhaps give a sufficient idea of the very varied nature of Cunobeline's types, and of their superior conception and execution as works of numismatic art. The coins are twelve in number, and about one-third of them can be readily traced to classical prototypes, either in their obverses or reverses.

Plate VI. The first three types in this plate are given as necessary to complete the series of the coins of the sons of Cunobeline as supplied in Plate I. The remainder of the plate enters upon the delineations of another series of coins, those of the Southern Belgæ or Firbolgi of Britain. Mr. Akerman showed, by close examination, that the reading of the coin No. 5 was, in reality, EPPI, and not IPPI.

PLATE VII continues with the types of the Southern Belgæ; and it may truly be said that such a remarkable series of coins is not to be found in the primæval history of any other country whatever, as those belonging to the said branch of the British Belgæ in this island, engraved in the present and preceding plate.

PLATE VIII. This plate supplies four additional types to the coins of the Brigantes, as given in Plate II. It

delineates two specimens of the Whaddon Chase coins
found in 1849, some hundreds in number, all imitations in
fact of the Macedonian stater; having a preposterous
head dress, wreath, and projecting appendages, intended
as decorations on the bust of Apollo, for the obverse; but
the face and features of the pagan deity are entirely omitted;
while the horse and his driver are given on the reverse.
However, there were some of the coins not coinciding with
the two given in the plate, but rather corresponding with
four or five of the types of the first and second plates of
Ruding's *Annals of the Coinage*. The last delineation in
the plate is one of the types inscribed BODVOC, considered
to belong to the ancient state in Britain which was named
the Dobuni, otherwise the Boduni.

PLATE IX. The first portion of this plate supplies
further specimens of the coinage of the Iceni, which, next
to the moneys of Cunobeline and those of the Southern
Belgæ, gives so much interest to the early annals of our
country. It has three coins of the main state of Iceni,
and two of the subordinate provinces. The lower part of
the plate is intended to enter upon the subject of the
origin and progress of the Gaulish coinage. The Macedonian stater of Philip II of Macedonia, No. 7, of which
we hear so much, is taken from a very superior specimen
in the British Museum, and is finely delineated by Mr.
Fairholt, both as to the obverse and reverse.

PLATE X. The three first numbers continue the subject of the origin and progress of the Gaulish coinage;
which is highly useful for the study of and understanding
of ancient Celtic coins of every description. The rest of
the plate is occupied with coins of a miscellaneous character, and with some others, five in number, considered
forgeries, or of a doubtful class, which it may be useful
enough to bring into notice.

PLATE XI gives mis-read coins, various *fac-similes* of
coin inscriptions, and two delineations of Roman family
coins, brought forward in the year 1849, by the late Marquis de Lagoy to illustrate the subject of ancient British
chariots.

BRIEF SUMMARY OF THE EXTENT AND GENERAL CONTENTS OF THE ANCIENT BRITISH COINAGE.

The following enumeration will give a comprehensive view of the whole of the authentic ancient British coinage, which, as given in this form, may seem rather limited in its compass; but the types under some of the heads are very numerous.

### PREDOMINANT STATES.

Trinobantes, Iceni, Brigantes, Dumnonii, Southern Belgæ, Riguantes or Regentes, Huiccii, Jugantes, and Cangi.

### CITIES AND TOWNS.

Verulamium (autonomous), Segontium, Camulodunum, Solidunum, Uriconium, Viridunum, Tincontium, Uxacona.

### CHIEFS AND RULERS.

Cunobeline, Vreisutagus or Prasutagus, Eppillus (supposed the Carvillius of Cæsar); Adminius, Togodumnus and Caractacus (sons of Cunobeline), Bericus or Vericus (a prince of the Southern Belgæ), and Vir Rex.

---

NOTES AND ADDITIONS TO THE CELTIC INSCRIPTIONS.

Pp. 35, 124. Vraichiauc, as a name for Mars. Camden, in his *Britannia*, col. 592, has an inscription to Mars under this name, found formerly on land belonging to Haddon House, in Derbyshire, and expressed as follows: DEO MARTI BRACIACAE OSITTIVS CAECILIAN PRAEFECT TRO - - VS.

Pp. 45, 58. Respecting the inscriptions, CORI and CATTI, on British coins; the one of which is usually applied to the Iceni Coritani, the other to the Catieuchlani, that is the Cassi; it is not perfectly clear that these two terms apply to any state or province at all. It is not mentioned that the coins CORI, are found exclusively in Lincolnshire, Leicestershire, and Nottinghamshire, which comprised the territories of the Iceni-Coritani, or that they are actually found in those quarters; while it is certain that the coins CATTI have been almost entirely discovered within the limits of the territories of the former southern Belgæ of Britain. Perhaps then we ought to look more closely to the obvious import and etymology of the words.

"Cor," in Celtic, is a place of worship; "cath" is a battle; CORI then may appear on çoins in the sense of priests, and CATTI in that of "soldiers" or "warriors." It is possible that some conventionality of ideas may have caused these words to have been inserted on coins. For example, we may suppose that the gold was supplied, in the one instance, by the priests to be coined in some exigency of the times, and so that the inscription, CORI, was appropriate; in the other instance, that the money was devoted to the payment of the troops, and so that the word CATTI was used, in the same manner, as RO . MI, and COHR . PRAET. occur on the coins of Carausius. This, of course, is only mere conjecture; and is given as such; but seems preferable to continuing to assign the coins, CATTI, to the province, or state, in Britain, where they are never found; and the coins, CORI, to another province, the Iceni-Coritani, with which we have nothing to connect them.

P. 91. The coin inscribed RVIIS, on a tablet, *i. e.* RVEIS VREIS or Prasutagus, described in the above page as found in a tumulus (called Muttilow Hill), near the Fleam Dyke, Cambridgeshire, was, in fact, found among the foundations of an old building at the base of the said tumulus, in April 1853, together with numerous Roman coins. It is engraved in vol. xiii of the *Archæological Journal*, p. 87, and in the *Numismatic Chronicle* for 1860.

P. 92. The *Regio* HUIC, mentioned by the ancient British historian Nennius, c. 70, of his *Historia Britonum*, would appear to be an ancient British appellation: in the first place, as apparently having a reference to the Iceni, similarly to the "Ordovices," *i. e.* the "Ard-Iccii;" and secondly, inasmuch as Nennius only mentions British names in the said chapter 70. There is, therefore, the greater probability that Huiccum is actually the name of an ancient British city of great antiquity; as is indeed implied by the coin of Cunobeline, which has VVICV on the reverse.

BERICUS or VERICUS, p. 123. The coins of this ancient British chief are only found in the Southern Belgic states; and as this fugitive British prince is

believed to have continued a ruling power to about the
year 42, it is evident that his rather ample coinage
must have been struck before that date. It is easy to
surmise respecting this prince, that being a chief of one
of the Southern Belgic states, he was chosen general-
issimo, on account of his talents and activity; and that
being beaten beyond any possibility of retrieving the
disaster, as is plainly implied, by the two sons of the late
king, Adminius and Caractacus, he sought refuge with
the Roman emperor of the day, and incited him to in-
vade the country, in which he himself joined cordially,
heart and hand.

P. 125. The following historical data are known of
Adminius, the supposed eldest son of Cunobeline. He
was in insurrection against his father, in the last year of
Caligula, A.D. 40 ; who, by means of another son, Caractacus, made governor of Camulodunum and his viceroy,
as the etymology of his titular appellation implies, *Caer-
vraight-tagos :* that is " the fortress royal commander,"
drove him out of the island to seek refuge with a few
adherents with Caligula, then with a Roman army in
Belgium (Suetonius, *Caligula*, c. 44). He and his party, it
seems, were made prisoners by Caligula, and marched off
for Rome, for the emperor's triumph (*ibid.*) But the
triumph being deferred, and ultimately never taking
place, on account of the emperor's death, four months
afterwards, Adminius and the prisoners were, of course,
detained at Rome till that time (Suetonius, *Calig.*, c. 49).
The emperor's death occurred the ninth kalends, February,
A.D. 41 ; or, according to modern computation, the 21st
day of that month. (Suetonius, *Calig.*, c. 58.)

Claudius, on his accession, it seems, gave a free pardon
to every one. (Suetonius, *Life of Claudius*, c. 11.) This
would have the effect of liberating Adminius, and it may
be inferred that he was received by the Britons as king
of the Trinobantes and Cassii, and that on his return he
began striking the abundant coins which he issued.

His coins express the spirit of freedom and of the
Druidical religion (see *plates* i and vi). It, therefore, may
be inferred that he was one of the British princes who
fought with Claudius on the north side of the Thames ;
and afterwards surrendered to the Roman emperor, at the

G

storming and taking of Camulodunum. (Compare *Dion Cassius*, lx, 20, with Suetonius, *Claudius*, c. 21).

The treatment, by Claudius, of the conquered Britons, appears to have been mild; for Dion Cassius uses the term, προσαγόμενος, which signifies that he "brought them into adherence." So, I conclude, that Adminius was allowed to retain his dominions; and that he soon afterwards, unable to resist the excitement which had sprung up among his countrymen, joined his brother Caractacus, during the remainder of his nine years war with the Romans, and at the conclusion of it surrendered a second time to his opponents, and was carried a prisoner once more to the imperial city. Ostensibly this must have been so; for when Tacitus tell us, in his *Annals*, xii, 37, that at last the emperor Claudius pardoned the whole party at Rome, in A.D. 51, the brothers of Caractacus are mentioned, and Togodumnus having been killed in battle long before, no other brothers remained but Adminius and Belinus. Compare also with *Annals*, xii, 35.

It was at one time in his career, as we find by his coins, that he took the name of "Aedd the Great" (Aededomaros). Aedd the Great, was a species of mythical character in early British history, supposed to have lived four or five hundred years before, and nearly occupying the same position as Romulus among the Romans; or as Assur, in the ideas of the ancient pagan Assyrians. As pride often goes before a fall, it is possible that this may have occurred only just before he was driven out of the island, by his father and brother, admitting that version of the account of Suetonius to be correct, to seek refuge as a humble dependent with one of the most ignoble of the Roman emperors that ever existed. However, we know not the time in which those coins were issued.

It is observable that the ancient British Chronicles of all classes invariably omit the mention of Adminius, though they speak of his brothers Caractacus and Togodumnus, under the names of Gueirryd and Gwydir, and Bericus, styled by them Lillius Hamo. Nor do the *Triads* mention Adminius, though noticing Caractacus and Belinus. The *Chronicles* we know were sometimes singular in their omissions of particular persons and events.

I assume from the prominent part which Adminius

took in public affairs, and his offering to surrender his father's dominions to the Romans, that he was the eldest son of the British king, and such was also Carte's opinion, in his *English History*, vol. i, p. 98. Carte also supposed him to have been king of the Trinobantes in his father's life time. (*Ibid.*)

There is some degree of similarity in the cases of Adminius and Bericus, who both fled to the Romans. Indeed they have been confused the one for the other by some writers, as by Horseley, in his *Britannia Romana*. It may, therefore, be required to specify in what respects their conduct and actions differed : for example,

Adminius fled to Caligula, in Belgium, in the year 40. Bericus fled to Claudius, in Rome, in the year, as nearly as can be judged, 42. Adminius fled to the Romans, to become a vassal king under the Roman empire. Bericus, to join in the invasion of Britain with an auxiliary force. Adminius, on his release, immediately rejoins his countrymen and their cause, and we have just entered into the details of his subsequent patriotic career. Not so Bericus: he joins the Romans, with an armed party of his countrymen, and was either killed in the first year of the war, at the same time with Togodumnus ; or, otherwise, at the siege and capture of Isca Dumnoniorum (Exeter), by the Romans, which must have been a year or two afterwards. These latter particulars, as in the *Chronicles of the Dunstable* class, where he is styled Lælius Hamo, a variation of the British name " Amwn," are of course dubious.

The line of the ancient poet, in Burman's *Anthologia*, 4to, 1759—

‧ " Libera non hostem non passa Britannia regem,"

applies to Britain in the era of Adminius; though the due explanation of the words is not known.

P. 148. UNCLASSICAL AND SEMI-BARBAROUS WORDS ON ANCIENT BRITISH COINS. The introduction of Latin inflexions on ancient British monies, has, without doubt, much softened the names, both local and personal, which are now found inscribed upon them : as Camulodunum, Verulamium, Jugantes, Ecenes, Durotriges, etc., etc. Therefore the legend QVANGETH, may appear harsh, and the legend FIRBOLG, may appear harsh also ; but let it be recollected that the first, according to the power of the letter ө, actually stands for QVANGES, a word soft enough. While in regard to the roughness of the second word, it can only be said that it is truly Celtic; and let a person look into c. 70 of the *History* of Nennius, where a number of British names appear, he will find that they are all harsh; and so are, for the most, the names of the twenty-eight, or otherwise thirty-one, ancient British cities which he gives.

Our ancient British moneys being comparatively still so unknown, as it incidentally appears from time to time, by misapprehensions in various publications, it is thought it may be useful to supply the following short view of the rise and progress of this science down to the present time.

---

## CHRONOLOGY OF THE SCIENCE OF ANCIENT BRITISH NUMISMATICS.

*(For various references and authorities, see Celtic Inscriptions, pp. 82-86.)*

I am unable to ascertain the earliest date when, or by whom, the term "ancient British moneys" was first used.

1596. Camden engraves eighteen ancient coins as British, of which, in reality, four are found to be Gaulish. The above were the first engravings ever published of ancient British coins.

1695. Bishop Gibson, in his edition of Camden's *Britannia*, publishes two folio plates of alleged ancient British coins, seventy-two in number, though, however, part are Gaulish types, and some approach to the class of *sceattæ*, and others to obscure continental types of the fifth or sixth century.

At the same time, Mr. Obadiah Walker, who had been Master of University College, Oxford, and had much numismatical talent, and indeed published, in 1692, a volume of coins in illustration of Greek and Roman history, somewhat in the way of Spanheim or Addison— this person wrote a treatise on ancient British moneys, inserted in this said edition of the *Britannia*, intended to be an accompaniment to the plates, and embodying all the learning of the day bearing on the subject. Accordingly, if we may except the remarks made by Camden himself, this may be considered the earliest dissertation on these coins.

1709. Gale, in his *Commentary on Antoninus*, p. 109, publishes the legend ic . DVRO . T . on a coin of the Iceni.

1714. Bishop Nicholson, in his *Historical Library*, p. 35, pronounces ancient British moneys to be, not coins, but amulets.

1715. Thoresby, a learned writer, supports his opinion in his work, entitled *Museum Thoresbeianum;* and Thomas Salmon, not long after, maintained that the so-called ancient British moneys, as engraved in Camden's *Britannia*, were brought over by the Goths, when they penetrated into the western parts of Europe.

1749. The Karnbré gold coins, in number about one thousand, were discovered, and are well described by Dr. Borlase in his *History of Cornwall*, the next year. They may possibly afford sufficient reason for considering that the Dumnonii had a coinage of their own.

1751. Wise, in his *Bodleian Catalogue*, published this year, thought that the so-called British coins belonged to France or Spain ; and would not own them for England. Wise may be considered the first numismatist of his day in the kingdom, being of about the same standing in his numismatic experience, as Taylor Combe was afterwards. Indeed he held a very similar situation ; the one being curator in the Bodleian, the other in the British Museum.

The revival of our British numismatical studies, from these depressing attacks, was but slow. Camden's advocates seemed defeated, and driven out of the field of discussion; and vindicators of any class were scarcely to be found.

In 1763, however, Dr. Pettingall published a quarto tract on the legend, TASCIA, of Camden.

In 1766, the works of Drs. Pegge and Stukeley were published, that of the latter posthumously. Dr. Pegge's work was his essay on the *Coins of Cunobeline*. Dr. Stukeley's, his *Twenty-three Plates* of ancient British coins, which were, however, without letter-press. Dr. Pegge maintained no more than the authenticity of the coins of Cunobeline ; while Stukeley's work much detrimented the subject by the bad engraving of the plates, and the numerous coins which he so freely introduced, Gaulish, Celtiberian, and others, which had nothing to do with Britain. A practised numismatist will, however, perceive that many coins of the Iceni, of various classes, are to be seen in those plates—many of our Weston and later finds, which had not appeared before, either in Camden's *Britannia*, or in Gibson's edition, or in Pegge.

Mr. John White, a silversmith, living just within Temple Bar, a brother of the celebrated Gilbert White, of Selborne, published his *Plate* about this time. It comprised forty-two alleged ancient British coins; but part, however, were Gaulish, and others of them gross forgeries, which did not mend matters.

Now about twenty years elapsed, when, in the year 1789, Gough's *Camden* appeared, in which the learned editor seemed to have shown himself rather careless in the department of ancient British coins; for foreign coins were much mixed with his specimens, and a number of forgeries were by no means wanting among them. However, a type or two of the Brigantes were first engraved in this work, and types of the Iceni, which had before appeared in Wise's *Catalogue*, and also in Stukeley's *Plates*, were again met with in this work and even some faint suggestions may be observed to be thrown out as to their due classification.

Nobody now had much to say for ancient British coins. They were condemned at home and abroad. Dr. Thomas Warton, a celebrated man of letters of the day, brother of the head master of Winchester School, cut them up at home, in a topographical work, and lowered very mainly their credit in the eyes of the world, as affording any basis of authority; and Eckhel and Sestini did the same abroad.

Ruding's *Annals of the Coinage*, published during this interval, though the engravings of ancient British moneys were very superior, counteracted but little the unfavourable impressions of the times, from the numerous Gaulish coins introduced, which discredited the work; when, in the year 1826, the Marquis de´ Lagoy, whose attention it is believed had been arrested by an engraving of a British coin, in a book he happened to possess, Gale's *Itinerary of Antoninus*, having communicated with, and obtained the concurrence of, Mionnet, published at Aix, in Provence, his *Medailles de Cunobelinus*, in a 4to. tract, pp. 20, and a plate. This evidently turned the tide, and gave the subject a footing on the continent, which it most certainly never had before, and possibly would never have had to this hour, unless the Marquis had thus given it his weight and authority, both of which were certainly considerable.

1836. A new phase now appeared in literature in England, in the establishment of the Numismatic Society; the tendency of which would, of course, be to bring forward ancient British coins into notice, in common with other classes. Accordingly, it was not long before numerous able numismatists came into the field, among whom we find the names of Akerman, C. Roach Smith, Burgon, and Hawkins, and afterwards of Mr. Birch and Mr. Evans. Mr. C. Roach Smith, in particular, much illustrated the coins of the Southern Belgæ of Britain, both in the *Journals* of the Numismatic Society, and in a subsequent work which he published, entitled the *Collectanea Antiqua*.

As we are now approaching so near our own times, it only remains to say that, in the year 1841, the coins of Uriconium began to be recognised; one being engraved in the *Numismatic Chronicle* of that year, at p. 152; one had been before engraved in the *Gentleman's Magazine*, for 1821, but had attracted but little notice.

1842. Mr. Alfred Beesley, of Banbury, brought forward his important ancient British type, inscribed QVANGETH, applying to the Cangi (see *Atlas*, pl. ix, fig. 2).

1846. Mr. Akerman published his *Coins of Cities and Princes*, comprising the ancient coins of Hispania, Gallia, and Britannia. This was certainly a volume got up like Mr. Akerman's other works, with much taste and learning, and had twenty-four plates.

1847. The Marquis de Lagoy ascertained the reading of the type AMMINVS, that is " Adminius" (see *Atlas*, pl. vi, fig. 1), which was the first type of the " Sons of Cunobeline " strictly speaking, numismatically identified, their coins having been before only conjecturally assigned (see *Journal of the Brit. Arch. Assoc.* for 1847, p. 234, and *Coins of Cunobeline*, p. 85.)

1848. The Record Commission published their folio

volume of the *Monumenta Historica Britannica,* with a plate of fifty-three capitally engraved British coins. The Record Commission in this volume, with exception of the autonomous moneys of Verulam, fell back on Pegge's ancient limits, of nearly a century before, of the coins of Cunobeline. Save, as above, they inserted no others, but the same class as his : and certainly they did right; for nothing prevents an author, intending to use ancient British coins historically, from bringing forward any class that he may wish, and illustrating it to his mind; whereas, the Record Commission, at that time of day, biassed by one and the other, might have, perhaps, at times made considerable and very undesirable mistakes of appropriation of the types, and this, it is easy to see, could not be expected to be avoided.

1849. A large find of ancient British coins, discovered at Whaddon Chase (see *Coins of Cunobeline,* pp. 169-70.)

1851. Mr. Birch published coins of Dubnovellaunos, that is, of Togodumnus, one of the sons of Cunobeline. See the *Numismatic Chronicle* for that year, pp. 74-76. For examples of the coins of Dubnovellaunos, see *Atlas,* pl. i, figs. 3, 4, and pl. iii, 9.

1852. A large quantity of British coins was found at Weston, in Norfolk (see Mr. C. Roach Smith's learned and very interesting paper on them in the *Numismatic Chronicle* for 1852, pp. 100-2). This extensive collection verified, with some few exceptions, nearly the whole of the coinage of the Iceni, the second state of ancient Britain, concerning which all doubt was now removed. It is right to add, that since the date of Mr. C. Roach Smith's paper, the termination ANTED, frequently referred to in it, is now known to read as ANTES, the final D being the barred D.

1856. Mr. Evans published coins of Aededomaros, that is Adminius, another son of the same monarch (see *Numismatic Chronicle* for the year, p. 155). Dr. Pegge had sought in vain for elucidations, and the two discoveries, conjoined with that of bringing forward the coins of the Southern Belgæ, by Mr. C. Roach Smith, were by far the most important which had taken place during the previous century. For examples of the coins of Aededomaros, see *Atlas,* pl. i, figs. 1, 2.

The same year, the coin RVEIS (*i e.* VREIS, or Prasutagus) was published in vol. xiii of the *Archæological Journal* (see before, p. 40), forming, at once, a decided step in advance in ancient British numismatics.

1860. Mr. Evans ascertained the constituent parts of the reading RIGVANTES, *i. e.* " Regentes " on coins, which name implies the state of ancient Britain, so called by the old geographical writer, Ravennas ; supposed to comprise the central state of the Southern Belgæ, of Hampshire and Wiltshire (see the *Numismatic Chronicle* for 1861.) Thus the coins are added of another ancient division of the island. The specimens in question formed part of a collection of coins, found at Nunney, near Frome, in the eastern part of the county of Somerset, and in the former territories of the ancient British Belgæ.

----

THE WELSH LANGUAGE, p. 148. This important member of the family of the Celtic dialects has one remarkable feature, *i. e.*, the change of initials in words, which often occasions the orthography of the root of a word to be as different as possible from the same word, in its different variations, as in common use. This custom has commenced since the thirteenth century, having been gradually introduced since that period. Its somewhat modern rise is undoubtedly fortunate for literature ; and particularly for historical research in the way of etymology, from which we now certainly derive such great and solid advantages : for had this custom prevailed in the time of Julius Cæsar, there would have of course been an end of all etymology ; except by a very difficult process. The origin of the practice might possibly have been from the upper classes learning and speaking foreign languages, from which cause they may have gradually shrunk away from a considerable portion of the vigorous and somewhat laboured pronunciation which their ancient dialect required.

LATIN LETTERS were used generally on Celtic coins, and Greek characters only occasionally.

ARIADNE. A predilection in the family of Cunobeline for names which had belonged to Minos and his descendants has been pointed out, *Celtic Inscriptions*, pp. 100-101.

It is undeniable: and the reason is believed to be that Timancius, the father of Cunobeline, exerted himself most strenuously in establishing, as a means of civilization, a system of jurisprudence for his country. Now, according to primeval traditions, Minos, the ancient king of Crete, had been extremely celebrated in this way; his fame for the administration of justice was very great; so that he was fabled in succeeding ages, in the mythology of the pagans, to have been made a demigod after death, and to have been appointed judge in the realms below. Add to this, it appears from the Commentaries of Julius Cæsar, *Gaulish Wars*, vi, 18, that the Celts believed themselves to be the descendants of Pluto, the imaginary deity of the lower regions, an idea which he says was constantly affirmed by the Druids. This must have led to a somewhat more than common worship of the infernal deities by the Britons; and both causes may have influenced the species of nomenclature which in those days seemed to have prevailed in the royal line in Britain.

We have had before the case of Adminius (see p. 100); and according to the ancient British Chronicles one of the Cunobeline family is found to be named Androgeus, of course after the person of the same appellation who was the son of the before-mentioned Minos, king of Crete. There seems, further, that there is another instance which, as illustrating Celtic matters, perhaps ought to be set forth. I mean that which is supplied by the name Aregwedd, which by some Cambrian scholars is supposed to have been a second name for Boadicea; by others, a second name for Cartismandua, but who, as most agree, was a daughter or sister of Cunobeline (compare *Triad* 22). I here just point out that we appear to have in this word another example of the fact which has been alluded to, that is, the name Ariadne in the Celtic form, "Aregwedd;" and Ariadne, we know, according to pagan mythology, was the sister of the before-named Androgeus, and daughter of Minos.

---

NOTES ON THE SOUTHERN BELGÆ OF BRITAIN.

The most casual reader of Cæsar's *Commentaries*, whether in the original or in an English translation, must have noticed that he mentions very particularly that he was opposed in his second expedition by four British kings or chiefs *in* Kent who made a decided attempt to storm his naval camp, but were repulsed. Mind I lay a stress on the preposition *in;* for I only understand that they marched into Kent for the purpose of attacking his garrisons left in that district, while he himself was pursuing his conquests further off in Britain. I entered upon this point some years since, see the *Journal of the British Arch. Assoc.*, vol. viii for 1852, pp. 12-14, and the *Coins of Cunobeline*, pp. 246-248; and the passage being submitted to the celebrated scholar and antiquary the Marquis de Lagoy, I had the satisfaction of finding that my views had his full concurrence in my thus translating Cæsar's words.

A very flagrant and discreditable error had prevailed since the time of Camden, and I have no doubt long before—for commentators, who are sometimes quite off their guard in their interpretations of an author's meaning and blindly follow one another, had taken it for granted that the four kings or chiefs were *bonâ fide* all rulers in Kent, and supposed accordingly that the county formed four kingdoms in ancient British times. Inveterate, however, as the error has been,—and there scarcely ever has been one more so,—yet this is one of the cases in which a very slight examination will clear the matter up, and, as may be very safely said, beyond all cavil or dispute.

It was certainly dignifying Kent very much to suppose that its comparatively small area should have supplied space enough to form four kingdoms: but as it is quite untrue that it did so, I must divest it of this honour, and leave it contented with that other genuine distinction that it actually did form a separate subordinate kingdom in Anglo-Saxon times. The fact is, that the words " quibus regionibus" of Cæsar, on which the erroneous idea alluded to has been founded, should be taken in connexion, not with Kent, but with his other expression which he previously uses of " Maritimæ civitates," *i. e.*, the Maritime States, that is, the Southern Belgæ or Firbolgi of Britain. It would seem astonishing that so easy an explanation as this should never have been suggested before ; but of course there is no arguing upon misapprehensions.

Thus, we are to understand that it was the four kings

of the southern Belgæ or Firbolgi of Britain who under-
took to guard our south-eastern shores against Cæsar, as
far as their ability extended, which service would
naturally have been suggested to them by the relative
situation of their territories. This south-eastern population we know from Cæsar was energetically seconded by
the other Britons.

The four kings mentioned by Cæsar were named Carvillius, Cingetorix, Taximagulus, and Segonax. I find
I assigned some years back the dominions of Carvillius to
Kent; those of Cingetorix to the Regni, or the inhabitants of Sussex and Surrey; those of Taximagulus to
Hampshire and Wiltshire; and those of Segonax to the
Segontiaci, or inhabitants of parts of Hampshire, etc.
(see the *Coins of Cunobeline*, pp. 246-248). I assigned
them so then, nor can I better assign them now. Indeed
there is at the present time apparently more confirmation;
for as Cæsar calls one of the leaders Taximagulus, or the
great chief, so the coins called the coins of the *Regentes* or
" the ruling state " now being found—and I sincerely regret that Mr. Evans had not been the person who completed
the discovery—accordingly, whichever the main state
might be, which may be judged to have been Hampshire
and Wiltshire, the same may be considered to have been
that of Taximagulus.

As to Carvillius, I have taken some pains to show in
the *Coins of Cunobeline*, p. 247, by arguments which I
think are nearly incontestable, that he was the same
person as Eppillus; and so I accordingly view that
matter decided. But again, if any one should prefer to
consider Eppillus to be the same chief as VIR REX, from
the coin inscribed EPPI COMF. CO. VIR. (see *Atlas of Coins*,
pl. vi, fig. 7), I am not prepared to deny it; though I
do not think it proved.

### THE CORNAVII.

It is mentioned in Pausanias that the Romans had
formed a native kingdom adjoining the Brigantes called
Genounia (Book viii, 43), which of course was founded
from motives of political expediency, to allow their armies

to act more freely against the Caledonians and other barbarians of the north. It is almost unquestionable that this kingdom comprised the Ordovices, or North Wales, with the Cornavii, *i. e.*, Cheshire and Shropshire, and the Cangi, that is, Derbyshire and Warwickshire. This kingdom was either established by Agricola or Hadrian, as according to Pausanias it already existed in the reign of Antoninus; and the Cornavii being the central state, their Uriconium was probably the capital of the whole province or kingdom, the etymology of the name being Gueired-y-conium, or the justice town (*i. e.*, seat of justice of the kingdom). This may account for the large extent and former splendour of the place.

Some few inscriptions have been found connected with the Cornavii, otherwise we are much in the dark respecting their affairs. They certainly want much the "vate sacro," *i. e.*, the commemorating poet, according to Horace's expression, or indeed a chronicler of any kind. One circumstance, however, comes out rather conspicuously respecting them, that is, the occurrence of various coins inscribed with the name of their principal city, Uriconium, which on many accounts form a very singular class, and are of great interest. I accordingly here supply an account of them in rather a fuller form than I have done in the *Celtic Inscriptions*, extracted from the learned and popular *Journal of the British Archæological Association* for April 1862, pp. 75-78, which was there inserted by me.

## THE COINS OF URICONIUM.

THE name of Uriconium, referring as it does to an ancient city of renown, is found mentioned on coins; and forms a subject which requires to be duly noticed and examined. The topic is one of interest; and as there are three or four varying types of them, it is my purpose briefly to describe them, in order that it may be understood what they are. Further, as this subject must be new to many, and indeed to most persons, I have to make the prefatory remark that these coins, which are all in gold, are of that class which is called "ancient British;" that the inscriptions on them are in the Celtic language, in a dialect much resembling the modern Welsh or Irish ; and that the word TASCIO which is read on them implies the same as the Latin word IMPERATOR, in the sense, not of emperor, but as ruler or commander merely, and is frequently so applied to Cunobeline, a powerful king in Britain of that day, mentioned by ancient historians ; and who, it may be inferred from these moneys, was recognized and acknowledged by this city as its sovereign. Further, that the name of the place is expressed on the coins by the word "Vricon" and its varieties ; and also that no other inscription has been hitherto found on any coin of Uriconium beyond variations of the above two words. I must now proceed to the description of the several types hitherto known of these moneys, with the readings of their inscriptions, to which I must request attention; as descriptions of coins, of course, consist of somewhat precise details, to make them available for historical purposes.

The varieties, then, or to speak more technically, the types of the coins of the city of Uriconium, as far as at present known, are four in number ; and they have this peculiarity, that though the lettering somewhat differs, the representations on them are invariably the same.

Having noticed this, it may be observed, that the workmanship of all the specimens is somewhat roughly executed, though certainly the figures are sketched out with considerable spirit. The obverses or front faces of the coins display a horseman with shield and helmet galloping rapidly to the left, holding some implement in his right hand, probably a carnyx or Celtic war trumpet, with which the leaders of the ancient Britons were often provided. He is looking back, and appears to be waving to his men to follow on. The reverse delineates a row of five spears, placed upright against apparently some framework ; and from one side of these projects another representation of the Celtic carnyx, or war trumpet. In all these specimens there is delineated a double tablet, terminated at each end in two peaks, and placed in front of the row of spears. On this double tablet the inscription is inserted in two lines ; one word in each.

The variations of the inscription are singular, as though only the same two words occur; yet the orthography of them is not always uniform, nor the position of the letters always corresponding in the different specimens.

The other details of the types may now be proceeded with, which are as follows.

I. Obverse the same as has been just before described; reverse also the same as has been just spoken of, and the words TASCIO / RICON in two lines. This coin was first published by the rev. Mr. Trafford Leigh in the *Numismatic Chronicle*, vol. iii, for 1841, p. 152; and is now, or a similar one, in the British Museum collection.

II. A coin engraved in the *Gentleman's Magazine* for January, 1821, p. 66. Obverse and reverse as before; and on the latter the legend TASCIOV / RICON. It is described as then lately found near Epping. This coin is evidently very nearly the same as Ruding's type which he refers to in his *Annals of the Coinage*, but does not insert, reading TASCIO VRIOON : the difference apparently being the misreading of one of the letters of the second word, and the variation in the placing of the letter v.

III. The coin in the Hunterian Museum, Glasgow, reading TASCI / RICONI.

IV. The coin in the museum at Rouen in France, reading TASSIE / RICON. This is engraved in Lambert's *Numismatique du Nord-ouest de la France*, plate XI, fig. 21, and is briefly referred to at p. 146 of the work.

With regard to this last coin, though given on good authority, I cannot but suspect the correctness of the reading. The o, somewhat obliterated, if such were the case, may have been mistaken for an E : likewise as there is no instance of a double s in the word TASCIO, the c, like the o, may have been misread. In short, the orthography TASSIE too much approaches to the form of a modern French word.

There is no question but that the name of the city of Uriconium is really of occurrence in these five foregoing coin inscriptions. It is true that in three of the instances the name is in the form of Ricon and not of Uricon ; but of this no great account need be made.

Uriconium, as a city of the Cornavii, a British state lying between the Ordovices and the Cangi, might be supposed, of course, to have belonged to the Iceni, and probably usually did; but the coins from their workmanship, which is essentially different from those of the Iceni, seem best assigned to Cunobeline, particularly as he was accustomed to strike moneys inscribed with the names of places which were, as it would appear, not within his usual dominions; as those ostensibly with the names of Segontium, Huiccum and Solidunum. The chances of war may, therefore, have thrown those cities, wherever they may have been situated, temporarily or permanently within his power, as may have been the case with Uriconium; which may have occasioned the somewhat transient, and rather rare appearance of their names on his moneys.

It may be concluded that there is not sufficient reason to regard these coins of Uriconium as "autonomous," which is almost the only remaining conjecture respecting them. They may be pronounced to be not "autonomous," there not appearing to be the occurrence of other types of Uriconium. In fact, they neither exist in number nor variety.

With regard to the weight of these coins; we have only that particular supplied with respect to two of them; viz., No. I, which is eighty-four grains, a common weight with Cunobeline's gold coins; and No. II, which is given us as high as one hundred and thirty grains: a weight which may remind us of the proximity of gold mines, which it is believed did formerly exist in North Wales.

I must leave all further discussions and inquiries respecting these coins to others, it having been solely my purpose on the present occasion to state the fact of the existence of these moneys of Uriconium, and to give a correct description of them, and some circumstantial details.

I cannot conclude without referring to the very spirited and patriotic explorations now proceeding at Wroxeter, on the site of the ancient city of Uriconium. These excavations, under the guidance, as they at present are, of talent and skill, may be looked upon as calculated to supply much insight into the manners and customs; and even, perhaps, by means of inscriptions, into the history of past ages. It is very possible, also, that they may furnish materials of a numismatic nature; and such as may either augment or vary the details of the coins of Uriconium given as above.

FURTHER REMARKS ON THE LEGEND VRE BOD TASCIA.
The coin inscribed thus, with which some uncertainties
have lately been connected; since the former observations
on it in our previous pages, has received, together with its
two cognate types, some further discussions as to its
authenticity in the *Gentleman's Magazine*, in several of its
recent numbers; and it, therefore, may be as well to
animadvert upon them. It is admitted that some forgeries have appeared in Suffolk; but I am glad that, as
far as the inquiries have as yet proceeded, there is nothing
to connect our present type and its two congeners with
them. Mr. C. Roach Smith, I observe, in the number
for May, corrects a supposition of mine, that the coin
inscribed VRE BOD TASCIA was found at or near Grundis-
burgh, and I find I was mistaken on that point; but I
now make some observations on another ground.
    I cannot view it as probable that a forger could have
hit upon the wording either of VRE BOD TASCIA, or the
same with the variations VER BOD TASCIA. There was
nothing known eleven years ago, in the beginning of the
year 1851, when the coin was first published, in the April
number of the *Journal of the British Archæological Association*, of any coin-inscription which at all approximated to
the words. Lord Braybrook's discovery of the type reading RVEIS, among the foundations of the old building, by
the side of the Muttilow tumulus, on the line of the
Fleam Dyke, was not made till 1856, or five years afterwards. We may be justified at the present day in saying
that RVEIS stands for VREIS, *i. e.* VREISVTAGVS, or Prasutagus, one letter being transposed, and the name VRACHIACA
for Mars (see Camden's inscription, in his *Britannia*, to the
god BRACIACA, col. 592); and that thence we have formed,
by British custom, the appellation *Prasutagus;* but how
could a forger at that time, in the year 1851, know this?
I therefore judge that the three types inscribed VRE or
VER BOD TASCIA are authentic, and not mere inventions.
    DR. PETTINGAL. It would be desirable, if possible, to
obtain some particulars of this writer, whose very original
researches on the legend TASCIA of Cunobeline, unex-
pected too when they appeared, at once placed him much
above the level of the other antiquaries of his day.
Feeling my inquiries would be somewhat incomplete

1

should I be able to record nothing respecting him, I have looked for his name in several biographical dictionaries, but do not find it inserted in any which have come to my hands. It is solely in the columns of the *Gentleman's Magazine* that I find some slight mention of this individual, and of others of his name; some of whom were, in all probability, connected with him by ties of relationship.

From this source it appears that he was appointed rector of the town of Newport, in Monmouthshire, in August 1739, which living was in the gift of the Bishop of Gloucester, and is then described as of the value of £200 per annum, and upwards. His works were:

I. His treatise on the TASCIA, published in 1763, which it seems was the substance of a paper sent to the Society of Antiquaries, of that day: II. Another work six years afterwards, thus entitled, " An Inquiry into the use and practice of Juries among the Greeks and Romans, by John Pettingall. Cadell: 1769." III. A Discussion on the Order of the Garter, and the legend of St. George; and IV. Remarks on the Inscription of Heraclea, in Italy. 4to, 1760.

His treatise on the TASCIA appears to be a full proof of his powers; his style being at once easy and unassuming, and he taking up a most intelligent scope in the line of his inquiry, and at the same time a very wide extended one; and, with all, bringing forward arguments quite new and unthought of before; yet so cogent and reasonable that no one could well refuse to agree with them. It is very true that he fails in his main result and conclusion, when it was quite within his grasp; but this might very possibly be from his great deference for Camden, who had laid down the law otherwise; and, further, it might be that he did not like to overturn any idea which was considered by the antiquaries of his day as settled and established. I follow with a few remarks with the same brevity as the above on Pegge and Stukeley.

Dr. PEGGE was one of our inquirers on the subject of ancient British coins. He died at a very advanced age in 1796, and was an F.S.A., and as such attended the meetings of the antiquaries, I believe, to some of the last years of his life. He is described as small in stature by a person who remembered him; but I could obtain no

further particulars that I recollect. His writings were
very multifarious, as appears by the list in the *Gentleman's
Magazine* for 1796, pp. 979-982 and 1081-1085. His
compositions alone, for the *Gentleman's Magazine*, amounted
to about three hundred articles. They comprised history,
ancient geography, and antiquities, and coins, British,
Anglo-Saxon, and mediæval. He even comprehended
cookery, in his editing the old treatise, the *Forme of Cury*.
He was a writer of the Goldsmith or Hazlitt class, and
as such very readable. As an author on the subject of
British coins, he was neither himself a bringer forward of
new types, nor a collector, but arranged, methodised, and
authenticated what was already known, but sometimes
not easily accessible, very successfully. He was contemporary, in his younger days, with Pettingal and Stukeley,
the first of whom he only once slightly mentions, and to
the second he disowns all allegiance (see his *Coins of
Cunobeline*, p. 106); while he brings forward specimens
in White's collection, certainly much to his own detriment (see his plate i, class 1, and see his work, as above,
p. 108, and his *Coins of the Archbishops of Canterbury*, in
the article of those of Bourchier.)

It may be noted as a defect in our national literature,
that no edition of the works of Dr. Pegge has ever been
collected, or his biography drawn up.

STUKELEY. This antiquary appears to have been of
ancient family and some fortune, and had the advantage
of good introductions, being patronised, as a young man,
by the Earl of Winchilsea of that day, and being a com-
panion of him in his tours. His biography never having
been written, but little is now known of Stukeley, except
from his works and incidental mentions in contemporary
literature. His acquaintance with antiquity was extensive; but I now speak of him in reference to British
coins, in which he generalized too much, but in treating
of which topic, contrary to Pegge, he brought forward
very numerous new specimens. He did so indeed;
though for the most part they were very carelessly examined, frequently misread, often wrongly assigned and
almost always very badly engraved. Add to which, there
was a considerable sprinkling of forgeries among them,
some of which are easily traceable to White's collection.

The publication of his *Coins of Carausius* was a great stimulus to the antiquarian world; and ever since has caused great attention to be turned in that direction. It seems that he also intended a work on British coins, as he intimates in his *Paleographia Sacra*, and had caused twenty-three plates of coins to be engraved, which were published after his death, in 1765. They were accompanied by no letter-press, and the existence of any written account was disowned by those who came after him.

Stukeley was much in advance of his age, but his assignment of coins, as in his *twenty-three plates*, is very fanciful.

About twenty years ago, soon after the formation of the Numismatic Society, his reputation became very low; and the late Hon. Algernon Herbert published in 1849, his *Cyclops Christianus*, in which he was attacked under that name for supposed mistakes respecting Druidical monuments. His authority has at this time become somewhat better spoken of, and he is now often quoted on British coins in a modified manner by numismatists of reputation.

# INDEX.

## A.

Adietuanus Sotiota, a Gaulish chief, 2, 3. Adminius, the British prince in the time of Caligula, information respecting him from ancient sources, 10, 13, 16, 28, 29, 33, 34, 39, 41-43, 47, 50. Aededomaros, a name of Adminius, 29, 36, 48. Agricola, the Roman general, 53. Agrippa Marcus, a coin of, countermarked by ancient British moneyers, 35. Akerman, Mr., 12, 28, 47. Ambactus, the Gaulish legend, its proper form, 10. Amminus, a form of Adminius on ancient British coins, 16, 27, 34, 47. Amwn, a varied name of Bericus, 43. Ando, 36. Androgeus, a name occurring in the family of Cunobeline, 50. Angora inscription, 27. Anted, or anteth, a termination of Celtic words, 20, 24, 33, 48. Antedrigu, asserted reading of, 19, 20. Antoninus, the Itinerary of, 45. Aregwedd, supposed Celtic form for Ariadne, 50. Archæological Journal, 49. Ariadne, legend of, among the Celts, 49, 50. Arivos Santones and Atisios Remos, Gaulish chiefs, 2. Arviragus, 29, 36. Assyrians, as also the Egyptians conjoin human and animal forms, and illustration therefrom, 22. Astikos, a Greek word in the sense of "native," on coins of Gallia Narbonensis, 9. Asup, a legend of the Brigantes, 33. Ateula, an ancient Gaulish chief, 5. Athenæum quoted, 1, 2-5, 8, 10, 11, 12, 15, 19, 24, 25, 30. Augustus, Roman emperor, 5, 9, 27.

## B.

Beesley, Mr., 16, 17, 22, 23, 47; his letter, 17, 18. Belatucader, etymology of the name, 5, 10. Belgæ, the, of Britain, how far they extended northward in the island; and whether they were Cunobeline's subjects, 7, 8. Belgæ in Britain, the southern, 4, 22, 25, 32, 37, 39-41, 49, 50; the midland, 7; the northern or Iceni, 8. Belinus supposed fourth son of Cunobeline, 28, 42. Bericus, a British prince in the time of Claudius, 28, 39, 40, 43. Betham, Sir William, 8. Birch, Mr., 12, 47; identifies the coin of Dubnovellaunos, 10, 29, 48. Boadicea, forged coin of, 36. Borlase, Dr., his History of Cornwall, 37, 45. Bouchier, Archbishop, a coin of his forged, 59. Braybrook, lord, 7, 57. Brigantes, a British state north of the Iceni, 29, 32, 35, 37, 39. Burgon, Mr., 47. Burman's Anthologia quoted, 43.

## C.

Cæsar, Julius, emperor, 5, 24, 49-52. Cæsar, imperator, family coin of, with trophies to illustrate ancient British chariots, 36. Caligula, Roman emperor, 41, 43. (Rex) Calle, the coin so inscribed, 28. Camden, 44-46, 51, 57. Camulodunum, 34, 41-43. Cam. Duro (coin of the Durotriges) legend of, 35. Cangi, an ancient British state, a rare coin of, 18, 35, 39, 53, 55. Cantii, the ancient inhabitants of Kent, 8. Cantorix Turonos, a Gaulish chief, 2. Caractacus, 11, 12, 14, 19, 22, 34, 39, 41, 42; forged coin of, 36. Carausius, 60. Carnyx, the Celtic war trumpet, 54. Carte, the historical author, 41. Carvillius, a British chief who opposed Cæsar's invasion, 28, 39, 52. Cartismandua, a British queen, 50. Cassi, or Catyeuchlani, a British state, 39, 41. Catti, legend of, 19, 35, 39, 40. Cassius (Dion), 28, 42. Cearatic, legend of, 34. Channel islands, coin of, 36. Chronicles, the ancient British, 42, 43. Cingetorix, a British chief, discussion respecting, 6, 52. Claudius, Roman emperor, 41, 43. Combe (Taylor), the numismatist, 45. Commios, Koinos, and Communitas, names of states in

---

*Works by the Same Author, in one vol., 8vo, cloth, price 10s. 6d.*

CELTIC INSCRIPTIONS ON GAULISH AND BRITISH COINS: intended to supply materials for the Early History of Great Britain; with a Glossary of archaic Celtic Words, and an Atlas of Coins.

*In one vol., 8vo, cloth, price 15s.*

BRITANNIC RESEARCHES; or, NEW FACTS AND RECTIFICATIONS OF ANCIENT BRITISH HISTORY; with a Map of Ancient Britain, Plans, etc.

*In one vol., 8vo, cloth, price 14s.*

BRITANNIA ANTIQUA; or, ANCIENT BRITAIN BROUGHT WITHIN THE LIMITS OF AUTHENTIC HISTORY; with a Map of the Territories of the Northern Britons, Picts, and Scots.

LONDON: J. RUSSELL SMITH, 36 SOHO SQUARE.

M.DCCC.LXI.